WIVELISC
CIRCULAR WALKS

Wiveliscombe Parish Council

Eleven circular walks from Wiveliscombe Square

From 1 mile to 23 miles

Take nothing but pictures,
Leave nothing but footprints,
Kill nothing but time.

American version of the Country Code

First published in 2006

By
© Wiveliscombe Parish Council

Printed by Character Graphics
Rear of 56-58 Station Road
Taunton, Somerset, TA1 1NS
Tel: 01823 279008
www.charactergraphics.co.uk

ISBN 0-9552851-0-0
ISBN 978-0-9552851-0-0

Acknowledgements

'The Lottery Awards For All' have funded this project for which Wiveliscombe Parish Council is very grateful

Authors

Brenda Boyland and Ann Scotter

Sincere thanks also to:

Frances Dransfield and Gillian Tennant for proof reading

David Impey for advice on publication

Geraldine Ingram for the pen and ink drawings

'Just Boots' and 'Wivey Walkers' for checking the route and script

Peter Sharman for drawing the maps

Somerset County Council for the O.S.licence

Any profit received from the sale of this publication will be used for reprints or funding walking projects in Wiveliscombe and the surrounding area

THE TOWN OF WIVELISCOMBE

Wiveliscombe lies in the lee of the Brendon hills and is a self sufficient rural community with a population of about two and a half thousand, providing all day to day needs and services. There is a range of accommodation for visitors.

The area was settled in Neolithic, Bronze Age, Iron Age and Roman times and Wiveliscombe is mentioned in the Domesday book of 1086 as a small agricultural community and first mentioned as a 'town' in 1179. It grew into a busy market town supporting the surrounding agricultural activity particularly the wool trade. Woollen garments were made in Wiveliscombe and sent to Bristol as part of the slave trade but when slavery was abolished in the 1800s the woollen industry declined.

The first brewery was established in 1807 and grew to become the main employer and there is a legend that Wiveliscombe once had thirty three pubs. Nowadays there are two thriving breweries but fewer pubs than previously.

A full, detailed history of this remarkable Somerset market town was published in 2005. *Wiveliscombe A History.* Susan Maria Farrington and the Wiveliscombe Book Group ISBN 0 - 9540992 -1- 4 (Colden Publications 2005).

WALKING WIVELISCOMBE'S CIRCULAR WALKS

The aim of this book is to enable this beautiful, little known, part of England to be enjoyed without dependence on a motor car by all ages and all standards of walkers. All walks start and finish in Wiveliscombe Square and most can be shortened by an earlier return to the Square.

The Wivey Way is the name of the longest walk. This walk encircles the town and its name is derived from the frequently used abbreviation of 'Wiveliscombe'. Not only is this walk circular but return to the Square can be made from many points along the route. The returns are described in other walks to which reference is made.

Walks must be chosen carefully as they vary in length and difficulty. The routes are described in detail and each walk has its own small map, drawn to the scale of 4cm to 1km (2$^1/_2$ in to 1 mile). The Town Walks and the Wivey Way are not to scale. All walkers are strongly advised to use this information in conjunction with the appropriate OS maps to which reference is made.

The timing of each walk is an assessment only. It allows time to admire the views and the countryside without rushing but does not include breaks for meals.

Distances are approximate and have been rounded up to the nearest $^1/_4$ kilometre or mile.

Walks are graded as easy, moderate or difficult.

Easy walks do not have steep climbs but may include some short gentle hills. These walks are no longer than 1$^1/_2$ hrs for the average walker.

Moderate walks may include steep climbs, muddy, rough fields and take up to 4hrs.

Difficult walks. Number 5 is the only difficult walk and this is due to the quarry.

Style - All walks are written in the same style:

a. 'Right' and 'Left' are emboldened to indicate that the route changes direction.

b. Points of interest. Numbers are used throughout the script to denote a 'point of interest' or 'short diversion'. These are described briefly at the end of each walk and further details can be obtained from the manuscript to which reference is made. The interest points within Wiveliscombe Town are only described in the Town Walk.

c. Lanes. There are several tracks in the area known as 'lanes'. e.g. Yard Lane or Coombe Lane. 'Lanes' which are a highway for all traffic may be referred to as 'metalled'.

Facilities There is only one pub and one shop directly on these walks. Others can be reached by a short diversion but opening times should be checked before leaving Wiveliscombe.

Mobile 'phone signal is patchy due to the hills.

The local taxi service telephone number is 01823 400009.

Bus timetables are available in Wiveliscombe.

WALKING IN THE COUNTRYSIDE

Please follow the Country Code:

- Respect the life of the countryside
- Guard against all risks of fire
- Leave all gates as you find them
- Keep dogs under control
- Keep to public rights of way across farmland
- Cross hedges, fences and walls at stiles or gates
- Take special care on country roads
- Leave livestock, machinery and crops alone
- Take your litter home
- Help to keep all water clean
- Protect wildlife, plants and trees
- Make no unnecessary noise

Liability

No liability can be accepted for accident, injury, loss or any other untoward incident whilst following these routes. All walks are on public rights of way and have been checked against the definitive maps. They have been walked by many individuals and are believed to be correct, but the countryside changes. Field boundaries can be altered and footpaths re-routed permanently or temporarily. Routes, which are clear and easy in good weather, may become slippery and difficult in wet weather. Walkers follow these routes at their own risk. Walkers are advised to wear boots or strong shoes and be suitably clothed. Due to the lack of facilities on most of these walks it is strongly recommended that sufficient water, food and a mobile phone be carried. Although most of the walks are on footpaths they can become isolated so ensure someone else knows the planned route. Care must be taken on all roads. Country lanes have their share of traffic and danger.

REFERENCES

At the end of each walk the points of interest are annotated A-G. This refers to the text from which the information is obtained.

A. *Sancti Stones.* Susan Maria Farrington. ISBN 0 - 9540992 - 0 - 6 (Colden Publications 2001)

B. *Wifela's Combe.* F. Hancock. M.A., S.C.L., F.S.A. ISBN 1 - 86241 - 009 - 7 (Esparto Digital Ltd., The Wessex Press 1912)

C. *Somerset Place Names.* Stephen Robinson. ISBN 1 - 87433603 - 2 (The Dovecote Press 1992)

D. *Mills around Wiveliscombe.* Martin Bodman. ISBN 0 - 9533539 - 1 - 5 (S.I.A.S 2000)

E. *The History and Antiquities of Somerset.* (John Collinson 1791)

F. *Somerset Railways.* Robin Madge. (The Dovecote Press 1986)

G. *Wiveliscombe A History.* Susan Maria Farrington ISBN 0 – 9540992 - 1 - (4 Colden Publications 2005)

CIRCULAR WALK NUMBER 1

Wiveliscombe Square - Maundown Hill - Washbattle - Bulland Ford - Challick Lane - Jews Lane - Wiveliscombe Square

Time: 3 - 3½ hrs

Distance: 9.0 km (5½ miles)

Map: OS Pathfinder (1257) ST 02/12 'Wellington' or OS Explorer 128 ' Taunton and Blackdown Hills'.

Features: A steep climb initially rewarded with panoramic views followed by a second steep climb up a quiet lane. Muddy in parts. Pheasants are bred and shoots are held in the forestry land. Dogs should be on a lead and children under close supervision. Good picnic sites can be found along the banks of the river Tone and cars can be parked at Washbattle or Bulland Ford. This walk joins the Deane Way between + and ++.

Grade: Moderate. Two steep climbs.

Roadwalking: 1¼ km (¾ mile) on lanes

Return to Wiveliscombe: This is possible at various points, by foot or car, denoted (**)

Bulland Ford

From Wiveliscombe Square face The Pharmacy/White Hart. Turn **left** into West Street. Take the first **right**, opposite Jones' garage, into a steep lane with high hedges. At the end of the metalled lane a driveway leads to Quarry Cleeve **(1)**. Follow the signpost on the right pointing ahead. Climb for $^3/_4$ km ($^1/_2$ mile). Ignore a track on the right + ** **(2)**. Continue to climb. At the road junction, turn sharp **left** and follow a footpath sign in the left hedge. Continue along the track.

Stop at the gaps on the left **(3)**. Ignore a metal gate ahead. The track bends right. As it bends left (100m/yds) stop at the bend and look over the gate **(4)**. Continue along the track for 250m/yds and go through the gate ahead. Keep the hedge on the right for 70m/yds. Then go through the first gate on the **right** into a field. Walk ahead.

As the field drops steeply look towards the right for a metal gate. Go through this gate into the forestry land. Follow the Deane Way signs ahead to a metal road. Beware of the traffic **. Turn **left** along the road to a track just before Washbattle Bridge **(5)**. Turn **left** along this track for $1^1/_4$ km ($^3/_4$ mile) through the forestry land with the River Tone on the right.

Go past the houses on the left and through a gate until a gamekeeper's cottage (where geese may be kept) is reached on the left. This area is Bulland Ford ++. At the junction with a metalled lane turn **left** **. Climb steeply, past a metalled track to Challick Farm on the left, then downhill to a rough track on the left (Kit's Lane). This is 1 km ($^1/_2$ mile) from Bulland Ford. Turn **left** along Kit's Lane **(6)**.

Continue 250m/yds until several gates are reached. Turn **left** through the 2nd gate on the left and keep the hedge on the left. Go through another gate and turn **right**. Keep the hedge on the right and go through several fields until a hard core surfaced track is reached. Follow this track ahead and retrace steps to Wiveliscombe Square.

POINTS OF INTEREST ON WALK 1

1. Quarry Cleeve, stone from here was used in the rebuilding of St. Andrew's Church in 1829. It is now a private property.

2. Views of 'Castle Hill', the site of one of the many Neolithic forts stretching from North to South Somerset. Roman coins were found here which can now be seen in the Somerset County Museum. There is a permissive path to the site from Castle Lane. (B and E)

3. Views of the Blackdown Hills and Wellington Monument. The field adjacent to the gate was the 18th century racecourse of five hundred acres. At the beginning of the 19th century the area was enclosed and divided. (B and G)

4. This is the top of Maundown Hill. Maundown means 'morning hill'. Views of Exmoor. (C)

5. Washbattle Mill. Previously known as Washbrittle Mill. It was mentioned in the Domesday Book of 1086 and became a fulling/tucking mill in the 17th century. In the 19th century it was a grist mill (for grinding corn) and finally it became a saw mill until the end of the 1914-18 war. During this time the cage for the Huish Champflower Church bells was made. The water wheel is now in the private house.

6. Panoramic views.

CIRCULAR WALK NUMBER 1

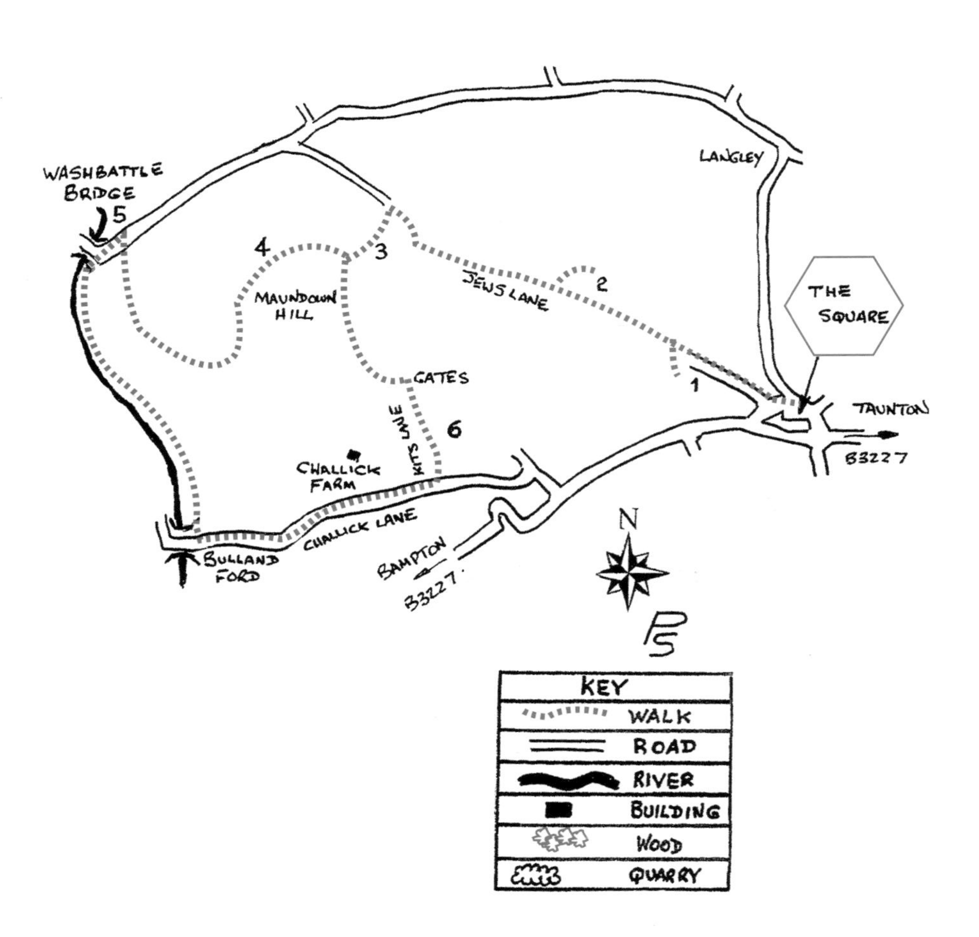

CIRCULAR WALK NUMBER 2

Wiveliscombe Square - Maundown Hill - Kit's Lane - Challick Lane - Bulland Ford - Waterrow - Hurstone Park - Waldridge Cross - Pyncombe Lane - Culverhay Farm - Wiveliscombe Square

Time: About 4 hrs

Distance: 12 1/4 km (7 3/4 miles)

Map: OS Pathfinder (1257) ST 02/12 'Wellington' or OS Explorer 128 'Taunton and Blackdown Hills'.

Features: Steep climbs along tracks, panoramic views, nature reserve and seasonal wild flowers. The Rock Inn at Waterrow, one of the few pubs available on these walks. Forestry land with pheasant breeding and shooting in season. This walk joins the Deane Way between + and ++.

Grade: Moderate. Walking can be slow in parts due to mud and ruts in the fields.

Roadwalking: 4 1/2 km (2 3/4 miles) This may appear rather long but all lanes are quiet with good views. There is the occasional car or farm vehicle and one major road crossing at Waterrow but visibility is good.

Return to Wiveliscombe: This is possible at various points, by foot, bus or car, denoted (**). They are not described but very obvious using a map or one of the other circular walks. The bus service passes Waterrow but check times before leaving Wiveliscombe. If only 'car' or 'bus' is mentioned it is because the road is busy.

From Wiveliscombe Square face The Pharmacy/White Hart. Turn **left** into West Street. Take the first **right**, opposite Jones' garage, into a steep lane with high hedges. At the end of the metalled lane a driveway leads to Quarry Cleeve **(1)**. Follow the signpost on the right pointing ahead. Climb for 3/4 km (1/2 mile). Ignore a track on the right + ** **(2)**. Continue to climb. At the road junction, turn sharp **left** and follow a footpath sign by the left hedge. Continue along the track but stop at the gaps on the left **(3)**, to a gate ahead where there is a sharp right hand bend.++

Follow the footpath sign through this gate and into a field. With the hedge on the left go through the fields to the bottom left corner of the last field. Keep **left** of a barn and bear **left** through a gate. At the junction of several gateways turn **right** down Kit's Lane, a narrow, grassy path, between hedges with views on the left **(4)**.

At the junction with a metalled lane (Challick Lane) **, turn **right** to Bulland Ford 1km (3/4 mile). + Cross the footbridge on the left over the River Tone and continue to bear **left** with the river on the left. A waymark is found a little way down this path. **Keep dogs on leads as pheasants are bred in the area.** Continue ahead, about 3/4 km (1/2 mile), to a barn and farm on the left. Turn **right** here and climb uphill.

The Rock Inn

Turn **left** at the junction and look for a gate in the hedge on the left. Go through this gate and down a track to another gate, then **right** to reach a metalled road. Turn **right** again for 1 1/4 km (3/4 mile). Ignore the roads on the right, and go straight on to reach the Rock Inn **(5)** at Waterrow **(6)** **(car, bus). ++

From The Rock cross the main B3227 and turn **left**, over the bridge then immediately **right** to the car park and continue on this lane, signed to Hurstone, with the river on the right. As the road bends left, in about 250m/yds, look right for a "V" shaped stone entrance on the right. Go **right** through this into Hurstone Nature Reserve **(7)** and continue uphill with the river on the right. Follow the fenced footpath through several fields. Walk on the left of a wooden seat and ignore a path going downhill on the right **(8)**.

Continue on the path **(9)**, which bends sharply **left** uphill to a metal gate. There is a pond ahead. Go round this on either side. Continue uphill with the stream on the right through a lightly wooded area. Up flights of wooden steps into a field **(10)**. Turn **right**, with the hedge on the **right** and fence on the left, to a gate in the top right corner of the field. Go through this onto the lane and leave the Nature Reserve **. Turn **right** along the lane and then **left** at the junction, and follow the sign 'Bathealton' to crossroads in about 250m/yds **(11)**. Turn **left** and follow the sign to Wiveliscombe.

Continue on the lane, for 250m/yds, to a barn on the left then go immediately **left** up the bridleway. Climb and admire the views **(12)**. The track descends to a metalled lane at Waldridge Cross **(13)**. Turn **left**. Follow the lane (Pyncombe Lane) as it bends right and continue for 1 1/2 km (1 mile) past North Down Farm on the right **(14)**. Then look for a footpath sign on the left, in the hedge, next to a gate. **Left** through this gate into a field. Directly across the field to a gate opposite. Ignore the track on the right and bear **left**, downhill, to the junction of tracks. **Turn** right.

Hurstone Art Centre

The direction is now straight ahead and downhill **(15)** across several fields. The path goes close to a house on the left, onto a metalled lane. Turn **left**. In front of the main farmhouse turn **right**, through a gate, into a field with Wiveliscombe directly ahead. Follow the sign downhill, through a small gate, to the bottom left corner of the field. Go through a kissing gate into a track with the recreation ground on the left. Another kissing gate leads onto the main road. Cross into West Street, which leads directly to Wiveliscombe Square.

POINTS OF INTEREST ON WALK 2

1. Quarry Cleeve, stone from here was used in the rebuilding of St. Andrew's Church. It is now private property. Maundown Hill is a derivation from the Old English 'morne and dun' meaning 'morning hill'. There are many legends, ghost stories and murders associated with Maundown Hill. (B,C and G)

2. Castle Hill is a part of a chain of Neolithic Hill Forts running from North to South Somerset. Roman coins have been found here and are now in the Somerset County Museum. (B, E and G)

3. The Blackdown Hills are in the distance with the Wellington Monument on the skyline. This monument affords wide views of the area but it is unsafe to ascend to the top. Wellington is associated with the woollen trade and the early Quaker movement. Taunton Vale opens up with Wiveliscombe in the foreground and the Brendon Hills rising on the left. The field over the gate was the site of a racecourse, situated on five hundred acres of land in the 18th century, with a circular track of two miles. After the Enclosure Act in the 19th century the land was divided and this heralded the demise of the racecourse. (B and E)

4. Panoramic views from Kit's Lane.

5. The Rock Inn, 17th century, where food and drink are available.

6. Waterrow, 'the water that is liable to flood' from the old English 'weter and hreow'. Flooding is due to the River Tone and the height of the Brendon Hills. (C)

7. Hurstone Nature Reserve has been developed on the farmland of Hurstone.

8. Venn Cross railway viaduct can been seen to the right, bridging the River Tone. This was part of the Taunton to Barnstaple railway line. The viaduct was planned initially by I.K. Brunel and opened in 1873 and was closed by Dr. Beeching in 1966. (F and G)

9. Hurstone Farm buildings are now an arts centre where several artists have their studios. Lectures, courses and open days are now held regularly. There are various objects of art to be seen through the reserve.

10. Hurstone Farm House is seen on the left. A mid 19th century building that can be hired for private house parties.

11. Before the left turn, look right towards a hill. This is one of the Neolithic settlements in the area and also the site of the Bathealton railway tunnel which was restored 2003/4. (E)

12. Panoramic views.

13. Waldridge Cross, means the 'crossways in the hollow' from the Old English 'wellrege'. (C)

14. The view to the right is of Milverton, listed in the Domesday Book as ' Milvertone'. The name, derived from the old English ' mylen weare' and 'tun' meaning 'The Mill weir enclosur'. There are some fine Georgian buildings and the church has some interesting bench ends. Taunton Vale and the Wellington monument on the Blackdown Hills are to be seen on the right. (C)

15. Wiveliscombe is straight ahead and the Quantock Hills.

CIRCULAR WALK NUMBER 2

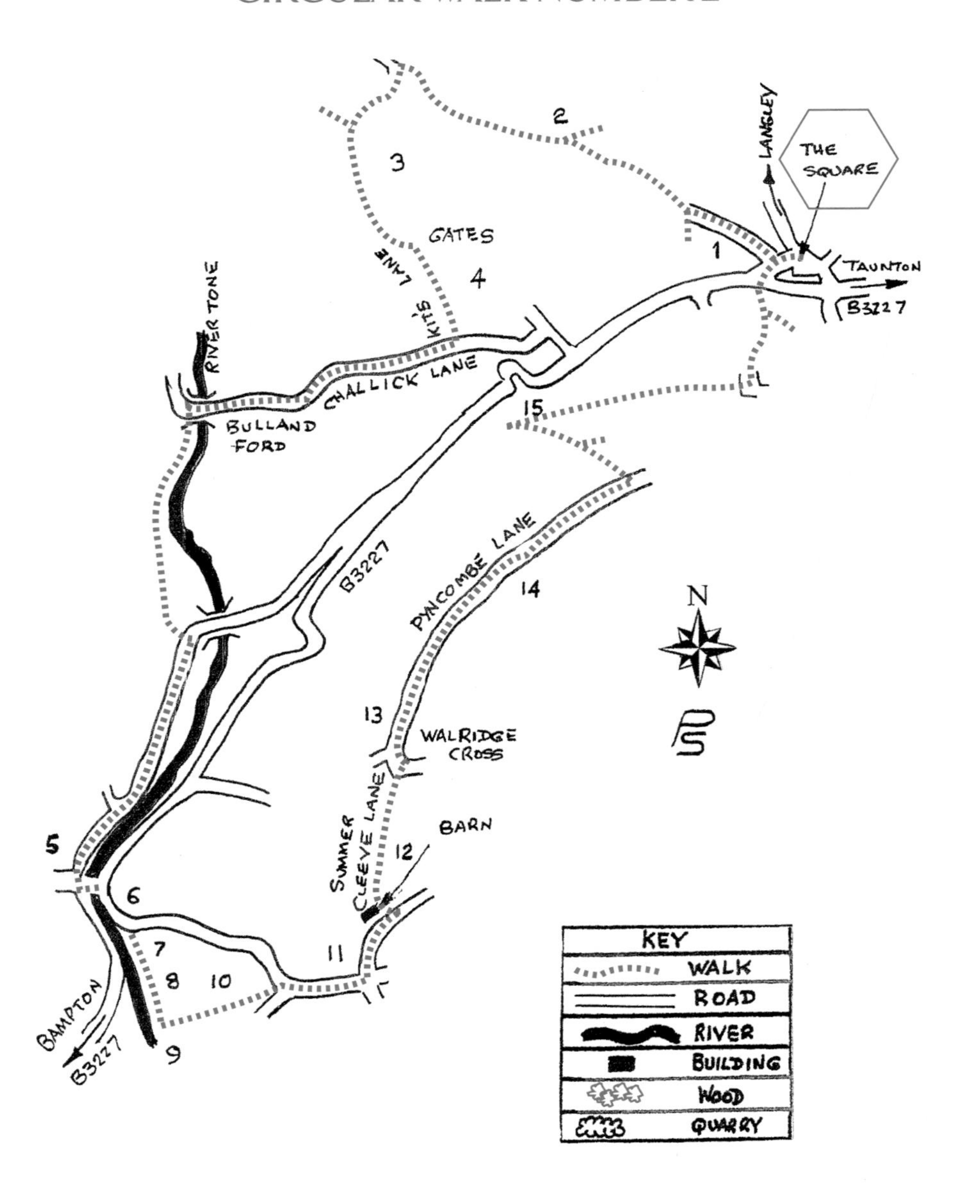

CIRCULAR WALK NUMBER 3

Wiveliscombe Square - Emborough - Quarthill Lane - Sminhay Bridge - Screedy - Quaking House - Slape Moor - Manor Garage - Wiveliscombe Square

Time: 3½ hrs

Distance: 10 km (6¼ miles)

Map: OS Pathfinder (1257) ST 02/12 'Wellington' or OS Explorer 128 'Taunton and Blackdown Hills'.

Features: Mostly undulating, no steep climbs. Quarthill Lane can be muddy and some of the stiles and bridges slippery when wet. Good views of Wiveliscombe and Quantock hills. Remains of the Taunton – Barnstable railway can be seen at several points. Quakers' cemetery 1681 on the route. Short diversion to Milverton.

++ denotes the point at which negotiations are under way to establish a right of access and public right of way over the railway bridge. At present follow the route as printed.

Grade: Moderate.

Roadwalking: 3½ km (2¼ mile) of which 1½ km (1 mile) on small country lanes.

Return to Wiveliscombe: This is possible at various points, by foot or car, denoted (**). They are not described but are very obvious, using a map or one of the other circular walks. If only 'car' is mentioned it is usually because the road is busy.

From Wiveliscombe Square face The Pharmacy/White Hart and turn **right** and then bear **right** down the hill to the traffic lights. Turn **left.** Continue past Saint Andrew's Church. Cross the road and turn **right** into Station Road, past the site of the station **(1)** on the left and go straight on, as the road narrows to become a track, with buildings on the right **(2)**. A stream and partly dismantled railway bridge can be seen to the left of a stile. Go over this stile and walk to the top left corner of the field. Then over another stile.

Follow the fenced path around Kingsmead School's grounds **(3)** to the end and **left** over a stile into a field. Direction is uphill and ahead. Keep the electricity sub-station on the left to a stile, which leads onto a road ** (car). Turn **left**. This is the road from Wiveliscombe to Wellington and great care must be taken. Follow this for almost ½ km (¼ mile) then first **right** down a lane with a sign to Richmond House Farm at a corner.

After a left bend, in about 250m/yds, the footpath forks **left**. This track, known as Quarthill Lane, **(4)** continues for about 1 km (½ mile). Then it bends uphill to a metalled lane **. Turn **left** and go under Sminhay Bridge **(5)**, then **left** again along a lane. Past three properties on the left. As the lane bends sharply left look for a signpost on the right, and follow it, **right**, through a gate to Poole Farm **(6)**. Follow the waymarks carefully through this private estate. Direction is ahead.

Leave a pond and hedge on the **left**. In about 100m/yds turn **left**, through a gap in the hedge and over a wooden bridge, which may be slippery when wet. Walk ahead, past a pole on the left, over another stream and continue ahead between 2 ponds. The path bears **left** into shrubland and passes over another wooden bridge.

Continue over the field ahead and some roofs will appear over the brow. Keep these to the right and go over a stile onto the road. Turn **right** along the grass verge, for 20m/yds, to avoid walking on the Wiveliscombe to Wellington road. ** (car). Cross the road and turn **left**, at Ivy Cottage. Continue on this lane 250m/yds. As the lane bends sharp right, look for a signpost on the left. Turn **left**, through a metal gate. The footpath is ahead to a stile opposite but it may be necessary to skirt left around sides of the field to avoid the crops. Go over the stile, which may be slippery.

Turn **right** to the right hand corner of the field and cross the bridge over a stream. Go over another stile and climb the hilly field, then through a gate, to the stile in the top right corner. Go over this stile **(7)** and walk along the top edge of the next field with the hedge on the left. The buildings of Farthing's Farm are to the right. Follow the track as it bends sharply **left**. At the junction of tracks turn **left** uphill between hedges. The track joins a metalled lane **(8)** **. Turn **left (9)** and walk about 1/2 km (1/4 mile).

Look for a footpath sign on the left and turn **left**, through the gate and walk across the field, slightly to the right, to a stile opposite. Go over this stile. Beware of possible knee-high electric wire on the opposite side of the stile and the use of electric wire in the next three fields.

Smimhay Bridge

Keep the row of four white cottages almost straight ahead and continue to a metal gate. Cross the lane and go through the gate opposite. Walk straight across the next field, with the four cottages directly ahead, and through a gap in the hedge opposite to descend to the bottom left corner of the field. Go through a metal gate and ahead into a small spinney. Cross the wooden bridge over the brook. Turn **left** along the bank with the brook to the left. Wiveliscombe is directly ahead **(10)**. Where the brook goes into a tunnel the permissive path turns 90 degrees **right**. Follow this to the main B3227 and cross the road **. The road is busy but this crossing point gives good visibility on both sides.

++ Turn **left** along the wide grassy verge and follow this in the direction of Wiveliscombe to the roundabout. Turn **right** into Nordens Meadow then first **left** into Lion D'Angers **(11)**. Cross this estate to leave at the top left, which opens onto the Ford road. Cross this and walk ahead up Old Brewery Road **(12)**. Follow the road **right** and then **left** before the houses of Cooper's Heights. The steep track uphill bends first **left** then **right** onto Golden Hill. **Left** to Wiveliscombe Square.

CIRCULAR WALK NUMBER 3

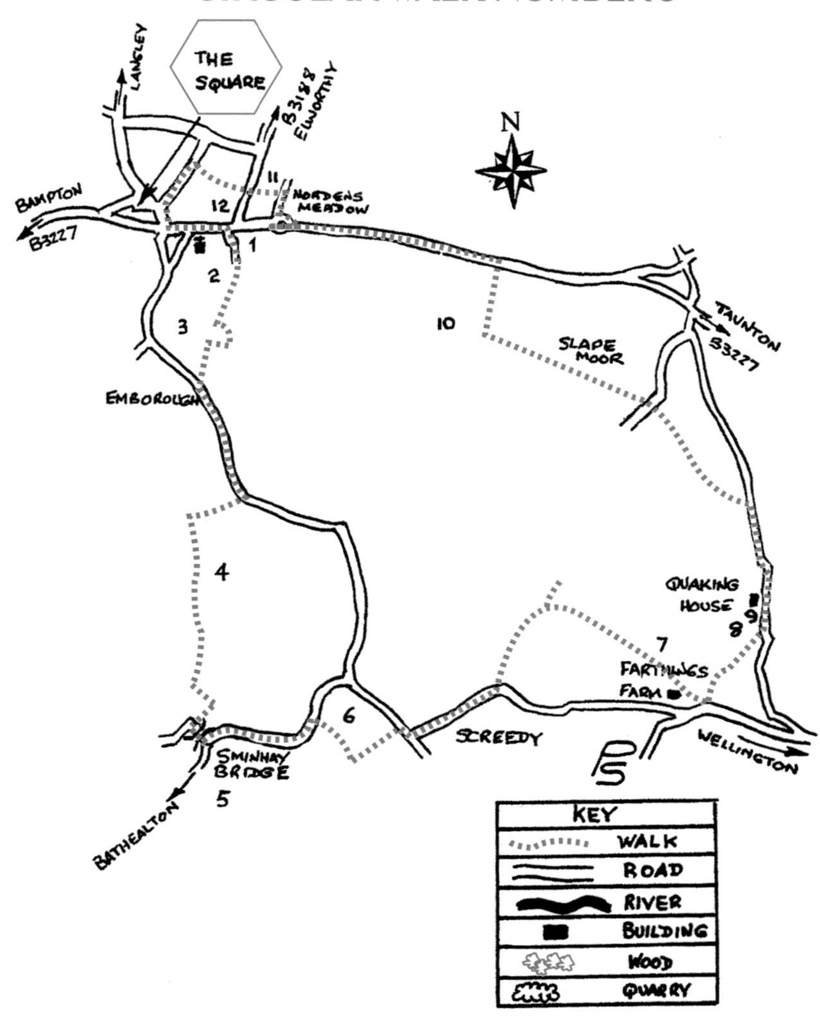

POINTS OF INTEREST ON WALK 3

1. Wiveliscombe Station opened 1871 closed 1966, the link between Taunton and Barnstable. (F and G)

2. Town Mill, originally a water mill, owned by Bath and Wells Diocese estate. Latterly a corn mill where locals had to grind their corn, raising revenues for the Church, now private houses, replacing a slaughter house, laundry and the mill. (B and G)

3. Kingsmead Comprehensive School built in the 1950s. It has a large catchment area for 11 - 16 year old children numbering approximately 800 pupils.

4. Panoramic Views of the Vale of Taunton and the Blackdown Hills .

5. Sminhay Bridge is an old railway bridge. People used this as a meeting place in the distant past. 'Sminhay' means investigation. (C)

6. Poole Farm is now used for private sporting activities.

7. Turn around for views of the south side of Wiveliscombe.

8. Quakers' cemetery, 1681, built between Wiveliscombe and Milverton as the Quakers were 'dissenters'. A local farmer, in sympathy with the dissenters, gave the ground. This cemetery remains in use.

9. Shortly on the right there is a signpost. This is a possible diversion to Milverton to see Georgian architecture and Church bench ends. (see walk 2, point 14)

10. The white building in the foreground is the local pig processing plant. Built in the early 1990s it is now said to be the biggest employer in Wiveliscombe.

11. Lion D'Angers estate was named to commemorate the twinning with this town in France. Exchanges have been made annually for the last 20 years.

12. This is a good view of the Hancock's brewery now used for various commercial purposes.

Chris + Nick
3/2019
Easy but take OS.

CIRCULAR WALK NUMBER 4

Wiveliscombe Square - Castle Hill - Ford - Cutthroat Lane - Wiveliscombe Square

Time: 1 hr

Distance: $3\frac{3}{4}$ km ($2\frac{1}{2}$ miles)

Map: OS pathfinder (1257) ST 02/12 'Wellington' or OS Explorer 128 'Taunton and Blackdown Hills'.

Features: Walk around Castle Hill. A short diversion on a permissive path allows access to this prehistoric site.

Grade: Easy. One steep field early in walk.

Roadwalking: $1\frac{1}{4}$ km (1 mile). Mostly on roads within Wiveliscombe or quiet lanes. There is a short distance along the road from Wiveliscombe to Ford, which is not busy, but great care must be taken because traffic can be fast.

Return to Wiveliscombe: This is possible, by car, at one point only marked (**).

From Wiveliscombe Square face The Pharmacy/White Hart and turn **right** then almost immediately **left** into Silver Street, which becomes Golden Hill half way down. As the road starts to descend steeply follow the footpath sign (which is on the left). Turn **right** up a concrete track towards the brewery. The track bends left and then right and steeply downhill to a small housing development, Coopers Heights on the left. Turn **right** then **left** to a junction with the Wiveliscombe - Ford Road. Turn **left**.

Just before Burges Lane, on the left, there is a fingerpost in the hedge on the **right**. Follow this track, known as Newton's Lane, past the housing development on the right. Go through a kissing gate at the end of the track and follow the well-worn footpath towards the pole at the top of the field. Continue with the hedge on the left to a stile. **Left**, over the stile and straight

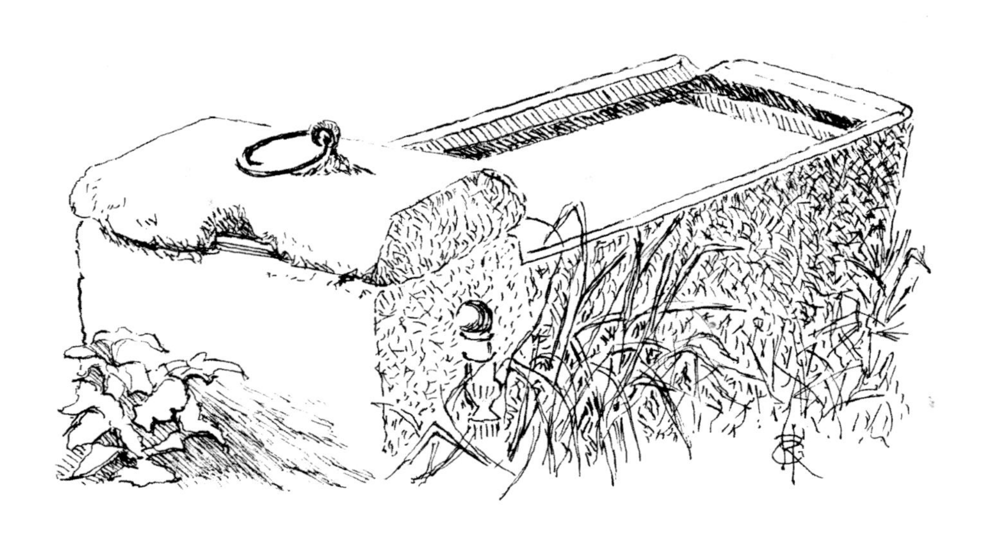

ahead with the hedge on the left. Turn **right**, to follow the hedge, but stay in the same field. At the junction of two tracks turn **left** for about 100m/yds. then **right** along a grassy track with hedges on both sides **(1)**.

Go past a barn on the left and through a gate. Continue straight on with the hedge on the right for about 200m/yds and continue through another gate to a stile in the far right corner of the field **(2)**, which leads onto a track. Turn **left**. In about 25m/yds at the junction with a lane, turn **left**. Past houses on the right **(3)** to the junction with the Wiveliscombe - Ford Road.

Turn left **(4)** for about 250m/yds, then **first** right in front of a cottage, Ford Gate Cottage **(5)**. In about 150m/yds (just before a bridge), turn **left**, over a stile, and through fields and three stiles, which are in the bottom right corners. The last stile leads into Cutthroat Lane **(6)**. Follow this lane to the road junction and turn **left**, then almost immediately **right** up Golden Hill and Silver Street to Wiveliscombe Square.

CIRCULAR WALK NUMBER 4

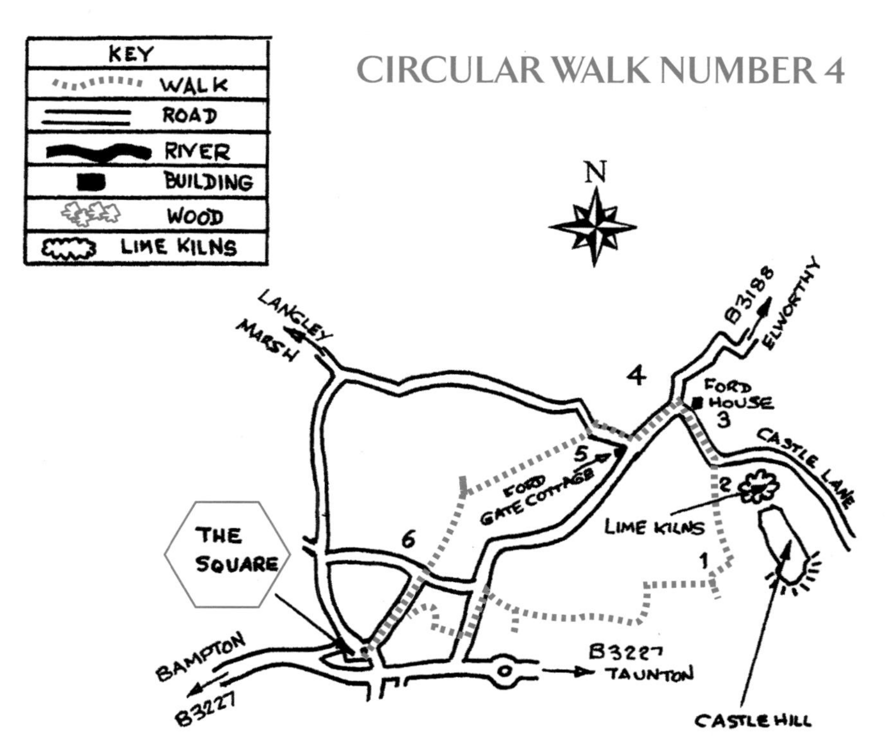

POINTS OF INTEREST ON WALK 4

1. Castle Hill is part of a chain of Neolithic hill forts running from North to South Somerset. Roman coins have been found here which are now in the Somerset County Museum. There is a permissive path from Castle Lane to the castle site. (B, E and G)

2. Lime kilns, restored in the 1980s, are on private land. Considerable custom was obtained from these. They were active until Welsh lime was imported. Until 1901, the lime was used agriculturally. (A, B and G)

3. Ford House was built by the Hancock family, who established the first brewery in Wiveliscombe. This provided employment after the collapse of the woollen trade. Descendants of this family are still living locally.

4. Ford. This hamlet once boasted 10 small farms and cottages and mills. Recently barns have been converted to modern offices.

5. Ford Gate Cottage. This was a forge and a tollgate.

6. Cutthroat Lane. Legend relates a murder took place here in the 19th century. On the right is one of two sewerage works of Wiveliscombe. At the end of the lane on the right, is the site of the Wiveliscombe Gas, Light and Coke Company (1857 - 1937).

CIRCULAR WALK NUMBER 5

Wiveliscombe Square - Cutthroat Lane - Grant's Farm - Ford Farm - Oakhampton Quarry - Coombe Lane - Langley Farm - Yard Lane - Cutthroat Lane - Wiveliscombe - Square

Time: 2 1/2 hrs

Distance: 6 1/2 km (4 miles)

Map: OS Pathfinder (1257) ST 02/12 'Wellington' and Pathfinder ST 03/13 'Quantock Hills' or OS Explorer 128 'Taunton and Blackdown Hills'and OS Explorer OL9 'Exmoor'.

Features: Panoramic views. The footpath is identified by yellow paint in the quarry. Notes about the quarry are under 'points of interest' no.6.

Grade: Difficult due to the quarry. The footpath descends steeply and there is loose slate underfoot without many footholds. This part is only recommended for experienced walkers who are wearing appropriate footware. This descent can be avoided by following the map on well established tracks through the wooded area to which the landowner has given access. (+........++ and italic script indicates alternative route).

Roadwalking: Less than 1/2 km (1/4 mile) on a minor lane.

Return to Wiveliscombe: This is possible at various points by foot or car denoted **. Routes are not described but very obvious using a map or one of the other circular walks.

From Wiveliscombe Square face The Pharmacy/White Hart and turn **right**. Walk ahead down Silver Street and Golden Hill. Turn **left** at the junction with Burges Lane and almost immediately **right** into a footpath **(1)**. Follow ahead to a stile into a field. Do not take the left-hand footpath.

Continue straight ahead keeping the stream on the left. Continue through fields and two stiles, which are in the bottom left corners. The third stile is also in the bottom left corner but is easily missed, so keep close to the stream and avoid going uphill. This last stile leads onto Grant's Lane **.

Turn **left** and over the bridge **(2)**. In about 100m/yds the lane bends sharply left but ignore this and turn sharp **right**. Follow the fingerpost past Lower Grant's Farmhouse and through a gate past Pitt Farm on the left. Just past the farmhouse look slightly left for a stile. Go straight across the field **(3)**. Keep to the left of the buildings of Ford Farm**. Through a gate and **left** onto a concrete track. In approximately 20m/yds take the second gate on the right and proceed half **left** across the field.

Look carefully for a wooden bridge, which vegetation may obscure, cross it and follow the direction of the waymarker (slightly uphill and to the left) towards the left of a big tree.

Over another small bridge and stile. Walk across the next field and through the left of two gates. Walk uphill with the hedge on the right to a gate in the corner **(4)**. Follow the track to the next gate and go through. At this point there are several gateways. Take the third on the **left**, into a field, and keep the hedge on the left.

The track bends left. Continue close to the hedge and go through another gate ahead. Climb the stile in the left corner of this field. Cross the next field and keep slightly to the right of centre. At the top of a slight incline keep left of an attractive 'shipham barn' for sheep **(5)**. The slate quarry **(6)** is visible, in the distance, a little to the left. Continue in the same direction over the stile at the corner of the wood ahead and into the quarry area. A 'caution' sign is a reminder that care must be observed at all times, with dogs on leads and children under control. Continue straight ahead until a waymark indicates that the footpath bends sharp left.

To avoid the quarry face *+ go straight ahead and follow the OS map through the wooded area which contains well-established tracks to which the landowner has given access to walkers. The direction is downhill and to the* ***left*** *until a wide track is reached. Turn* ***left*** *and look for a low red cautionary sign on the right in about 250m/yds Turn* ***sharply*** *right to complete the quarry descent. This is narrow and steep ++ .*

To continue Walk 5 down the main quarry face follow the marked path into a clearing. (Do not turn right at this point as this path drops into the quarry in a short distance). The footpath continues ahead. The direction is in line with a cottage in the valley and is steeply downhill.

It can be hazardous due to loose slate. Extreme caution is required here until a wide flat path is reached.

The Quarry

Turn **right** and follow the track until a waymark (on a low metal sign) is seen on the left. Turn **left** and descend steeply. ++ Care must still be exercised. At the bottom of the quarry cross the stream and stile. Keep the hedge on the right. Go over the stile in the top right corner of the field. Turn **left** along the track until a stream is seen on the right. This stream usually floods the track.

Go over the footbridge, on the **right**, just before the flood is reached. Then scramble up to a second stile with a waymark, which points to the top right - hand corner of the next field. Climb this steep field and go over a stile into a track, known as Deepleigh Lane. Walk down the track ahead. In about 100m/yds, follow the waymark through a gate into a field. Continue downhill, close to a hedge on the right. The path bends left and ascends slightly past an animal shed on the left **.

Straight across the metalled lane, Grant's Lane, to a track, known as Yard Lane, and follow the fingerpost for 200m/yds to a stile. **Right**, and descend through two fields to stiles in the bottom right corners. Follow the waymark half left in the next field. This field may be waterlogged and rough. The path is reinforced over the stream. Go over a stile into the next field then the final stile is a short distance on the **right**. Retrace steps through Cutthroat Lane and Golden Hill to Wiveliscombe Square.

POINTS OF INTEREST ON WALK 5

1. Cutthroat Lane. Legend relates a murder took place here in the 19th century. The site of Wiveliscombe Gas, Coke and Light Company, (1857 - 1937), is on the left. The gasometer was removed in 1966. One of the two sewerage works of Wiveliscombe is at the end of this lane on the left.

2. In previous years a channel was made here, on the right hand side of the bridge, to dip sheep.

3. The hill on the right is known as 'Castle Hill' the site of one of many Neolithic forts stretching from North to South Somerset. Roman coins were found here which are now in the Somerset County Museum. There is a permissive path to the site from Castle Lane. (B, D and G)

4. Turn around, lean on the gate and look at the views.

5. The 'Shipham' from the Old English 'scip and ham' means 'Sheep's house'. (C)

6. Oakhampton Quarry. In 1608 the Dean and Chapter of Wells granted a lease to the Manor of Oakhampton, to develop the slate quarry. The churchwardens' accounts show large quantities of slate were sold to the church for the roof. Alas this slate was soft, nowadays imported slate is used. There is evidence of local slate to be seen in the floor of the Church.
(B and G)

CIRCULAR WALK NUMBER 5

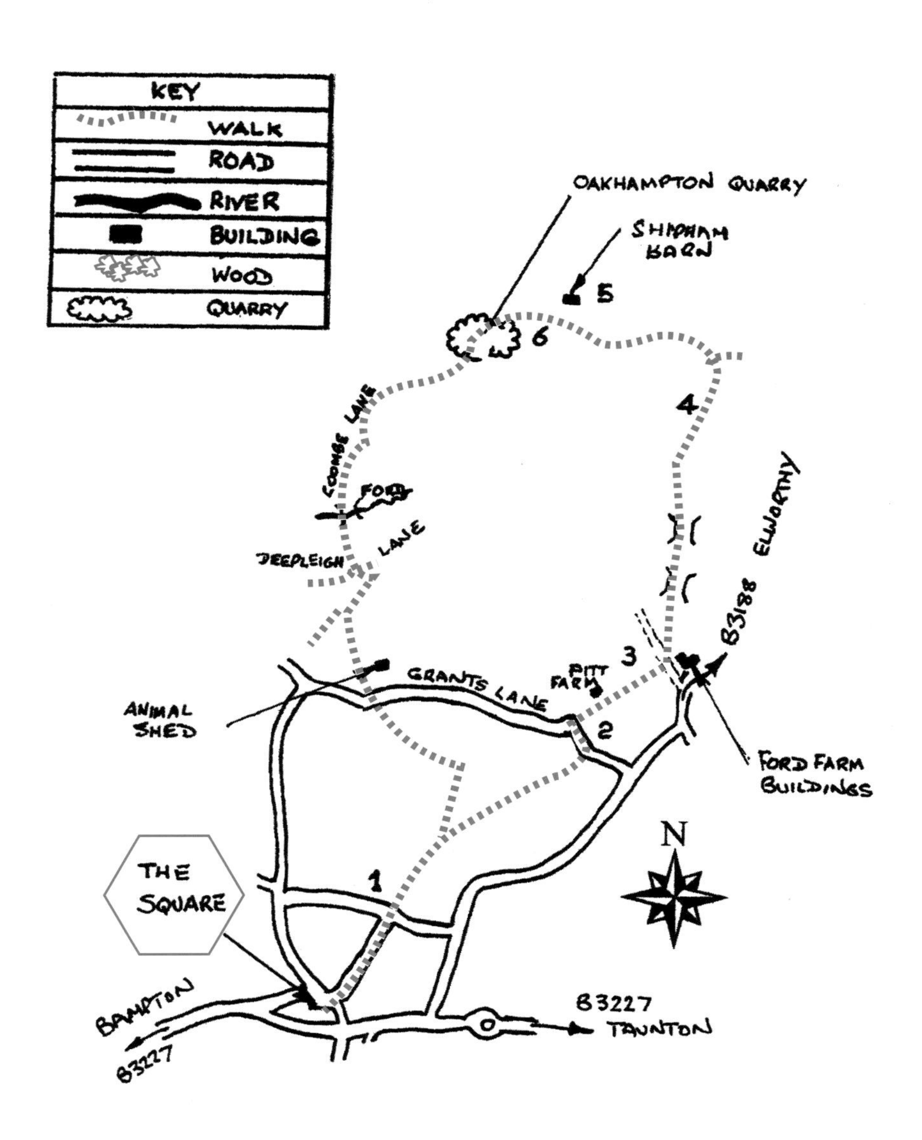

CIRCULAR WALK NUMBER 6

Wiveliscombe Square - Langley Cross - Coombe Lane - Brompton Ralph - Wescott Farm - Bowden Farm - Cording's Farm - Whitefield - Coombe Lane - Langley Farm - Yard Lane - Cutthroat Lane - Golden Hill - Wiveliscombe Square

Time: 3$^1/_2$ to 4 hrs

Distance: 12 km (7$^1/_2$ miles)

Map: OS Pathfinder (1257) ST 02/12 'Wellington' and OS Pathfinder ST 03/13 'Quantock Hills' or OS Explorer 128 'Taunton and Blackdown Hills' and OS Explorer OL9 'Exmoor'.

Features: Attractive wooded valley to Brompton Ralph. Village shop open in the mornings. Open pastureland with panoramic views. Part of this walk follows The Deane Way between +......++.

Grade: Moderate / Difficult. The final section of Coombe Lane, joined at Whitefield, can be very slippery even in dry weather. There are flat rocks beneath the surface and care must be taken along this track. This section can be avoided by following the road back to Wiveliscombe. # denotes this point.

Roadwalking: 1$^1/_4$ km ($^3/_4$ mile) within Wiveliscombe and 1$^1/_2$ km (1 mile) on country lanes.

Return to Wiveliscombe: This is possible at various points by foot or car denoted **. Routes are not described but very obvious using a map or one of the other circular walks.

From Wiveliscombe Square face The Pharmacy/White Hart and walk ahead on the right hand side of North Street, past the Bear Inn on the right and the Victorian Primary School on the left. When the pavement ends, in about 1km ($^3/_4$ mile), cross the road and continue on the other side.

Pool Mill

Brompton Ralph

Walk on the raised path past the houses on the left, then go through the second gate on the right, just before the path ends. Cross the road and walk up the footpath ahead, known as Sandy Lane **(1)**. Climb for 250m/yds to a wide junction **(2)**. Follow the fingerpost opposite, climb the stile into the field ahead, and descend steeply. Keep the hedge on the left and go over stiles at the bottom of the field. Go over the stream and **left** up a track known as Coombe Lane. This may resemble a small stream after rain. In 250m/yds, after a downward bend, go over a stile on the **right**. Walk ahead and keep the hedge on the left.

Pass through a "V" stile and over a bridge. Turn **left** and keep the river on the left. There are several paths in this woodland, all of which are permissive. They all reach the same end point in $1\frac{3}{4}$ km (1 mile) but it is probably easiest to keep within the wooded area and certainly do not cross the river **(3)**.

Turn **left** on the metalled lane to Brompton Ralph **(4)**. Keep **left** at the Village Green and continue $\frac{3}{4}$ km ($\frac{1}{2}$ mile). Turn **left** to Westcott Farm. Before the farm turn **right** through a gate. Keep the farmhouse on the left and through another gate into a field. Continue ahead with the hedge and young woodland on the right. Through a gate in the right-hand corner of this field. Cross the track and through another gate, to skirt the back of Leigh Cottages on the left.

Go through the gate and turn **left**. Through another gate into a field. Turn **right**. Keep the hedge on the right to a gate in the right-hand corner of the field. Go diagonally across this long field to the far left corner and cross the small stream. Walk up the track, through a gate, and ahead to Bowden Farm **(5)**.

Go through the farmyard and track to a metalled lane. Turn **left** for 250m/yds and **left** again through the first gate into a field. Climb uphill and half **right** to a stile at the top of the field. Keep the hedge on the left through the next three fields to the driveway of Cording's Farm. Cross this drive, climb the stile opposite and **left**. Keep the hedge on the right. In the next field keep the hedge on the left to the bottom corner.

Go over a stile onto a metalled road, and turn **left** for 250m/yds #. Turn **left** again, onto the bridleway, at Whitefield Farm. In about 25m/yds go through a gate ahead and down the track with high hedges on both sides. This track is Coombe Lane. Rocks underfoot can be very slippery in all weathers for most of this track. Continue for 1½ km (1 mile), until a stream is seen on the right.

This stream usually floods the track. Go over the footbridge, on the **right**, just before the flood is reached. Then scramble up to a second stile with a waymark, which points to the top right - hand corner of the next field. Climb this steep field and go over a stile into a track, known as Deepleigh Lane. Walk down the track ahead. In 200m/yds, follow the waymark through a gate into a field. Continue downhill, close to a hedge on the right.

The path bends left and ascends slightly past an animal shed on the left **. Straight across the metalled lane to a track, known as Yard Lane, and follow the fingerpost for 250m/yds to a stile. Go over this stile and immediately **right**, and descend through two fields to stiles in the bottom right corners.

Follow the waymark half **left** in the next field. This field may be waterlogged and rough. The path is reinforced over the stream. Go over a stile into the next field then the final stile is a short distance on the **right**. Retrace steps through Cutthroat Lane and Golden Hill to Wiveliscombe Square.

POINTS OF INTEREST ON WALK 6

1. This was the road from Oakhampton Quarry, steep sided and originally cobbled. Horse drawn carts would have brought the slate along this track.

2. Oakhampton Quarry. In 1608 the Dean and Chapter of Wells granted a lease to the Manor of Oakhampton to develop the quarry. The Churchwardens' accounts show large quantities of slate were sold to the church for the roof. Alas this slate was soft. Today imported slate is used. Some of the machinery used in the quarry is submerged at the base. (B and G)

3. Pool Mill (1799 - 1894), the ruins may be seen on the left, it was a 'water grist mill', the site being cleared in the early 1980's leaving only the mill house. (D and G)

4. Brompton Ralph is listed in the Domesday Book of 1086 as 'Brunetune', in old English, this means, 'the shrub broom enclosure' from ' brom' and 'tun'. The community runs the general store and Post Office. This is open until 1p.m. The green is an ideal spot to picnic, with a seat under the tree. (C)

5. Bowden Farm means in Old English the farm on the curved hill'. (C)

CIRCULAR WALK NUMBER 6

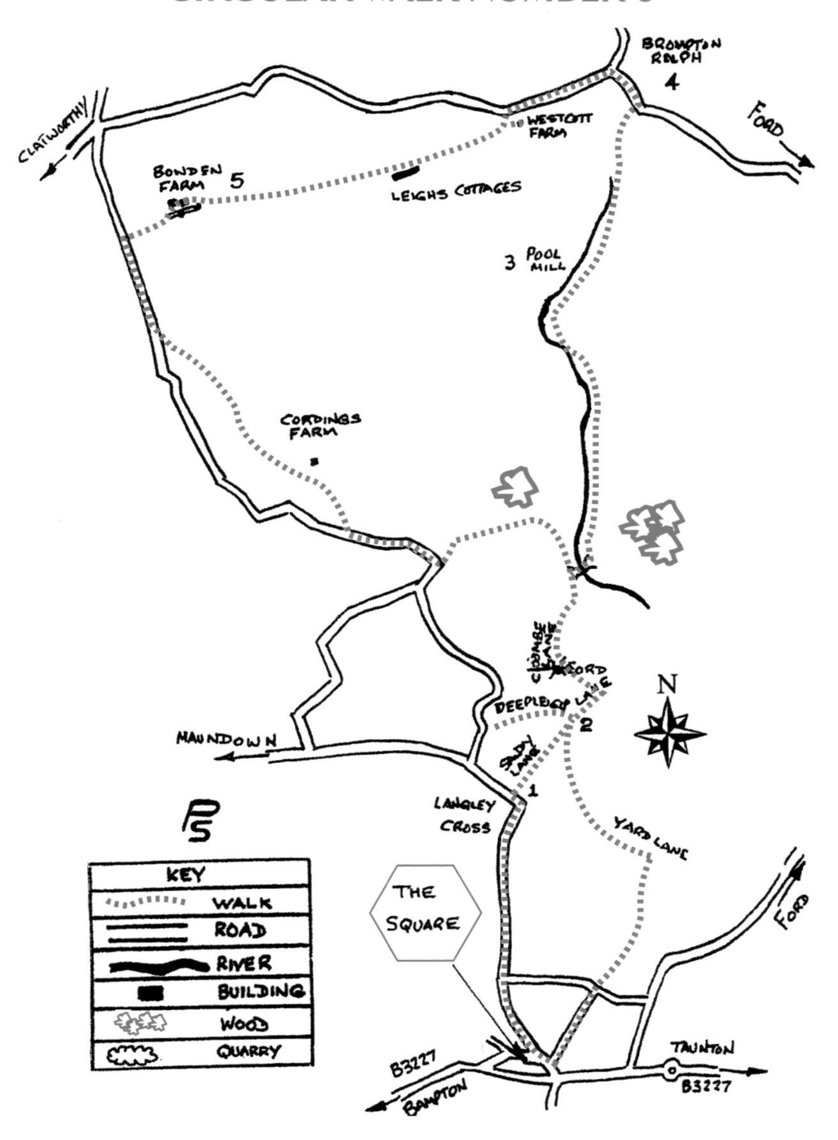

CIRCULAR WALK NUMBER 7

Wiveliscombe Square - Langley - Langley Marsh - Jews Farm - Tuck Mill Copse - Maundown Dairy Farm - Maundown Hill - Wiveliscombe Square

Time: 2 1/2 to 3 hrs

Distance: 8 1/4 km (5 1/4 miles)

Map: OS Pathfinder (1257) ST 02/12 'Wellington' or OS Explorer 128 'Taunton and Blackdown Hills'.

Features: Mostly paths through agricultural, equine or horticultural land. Hilly in parts. Views of Maundown Hill and a short diversion to Huish Champflower marked *. (see The Wivey Way points of interest 10 and 11)

Grade: Moderate.

Roadwalking: 1 1/4 km (3/4 mile) on the pavement of the road out of Wiveiscombe. 1 km (1/2 mile) on very quiet lanes.

Return to Wiveliscombe: This is possible at various points by foot or car denoted **. The routes are not described but are very obvious using a map or one of the other circular walks.

From Wiveliscombe Square face the Pharmacy/White Hart and walk ahead along North Street, past the Bear Inn on the right and the Victorian Primary School on the left. When the right hand pavement ends, in about 1 km (1/2 mile), walk on the left. Turn **left**, just before the red brick houses, along a service road. In about 25m/yds, go through the gateway ahead into a field. Keep the hedge on the left, go through a gateway, and cross a small stream, then keep the hedge on the right **(1)**.

St Luke's Church

Continue across the field and through a gateway, past back gardens of houses on the right to a gate in the hedge opposite. This gate opens onto a path which bends right between the houses to a road **. Turn **left** uphill for about 1/2 km (1/4mile). Go over a stile on the **right**. Follow the waymarks through a series of gates. Walk past the horses with due care. Continue slightly **left** and downhill to a stile in the bottom left corner. Go through a small spinney, over a stile, and a bridge.

Climb, slightly to the **left**, across the field, past a post, to a stile in the top left corner. Go over the stile, head up the field and through a gate at the top. Turn immediately **right** through another gate and cross the field to a stile in the left hedge. This leads into a beautiful private garden. Continue ahead (through the garden) keep the house on the left and greenhouse on the right.

Climb over the stile ahead, past a shed and house close (on the right) into a metalled lane **. Cross this lane into the driveway of Jews Farm. Go past the house on the left, to a gate, onto a track. Turn **left**. The houses and farm buildings are on the left. Go through two more gates into a field. Go across the first field to a gate. Walk slightly to the **left** across the next field, with Huish Champflower Church **(2)** directly ahead, then through the left of two gates. Walk ahead through the next field, which may have a small stream in the middle of it, and do not descend the hill to the bottom.

Go through a metal gate into a gorse thicket. The path leads downhill through a wooded area for less than 250m/yds.

***Diversion to Huish Champflower**

The path continuing the walk is difficult to find. Turn very sharply **left** and downhill. There is a waymark, after about 15m/yds low on a tree on the right. (If the stream, bridge and a ruined house, which is Tuck Mill, are reached **(3)**, retrace steps to find the path).

Continue through the spinney with the stream on the right. The narrow path leads over two stiles and a gate into a field. Continue ahead, through the middle of a long field and through a gateway in the far bottom right-hand corner. Cross the small stream and go up the next field with a row of trees and rocks on the right.

Walk ahead, through a metal gate. Continue up the hill with the hedge on the right for about 50m/yds and go over the double stile into the next field. Keep the hedge on the left and follow the path as it bends left. Go over the stile, in the bottom left corner of the field, onto a metalled lane **(4)****. Turn **right** to the road junction and **right** again up the road. Turn **left**, up the metalled lane, to the top of the hill. Fork **left**, along the bridleway, downhill. Fork **right** after about 1/2 km (1/4 mile) and continue to Wiveliscombe Square.

POINTS OF INTEREST ON WALK 7

1. St Luke's Church, Langley Marsh, is seen on the right. A 'flat packed' church made of corrugated iron sheeting and lined with wood. Erected in the 1890s for the 'religious education of the poor, notably children'. This is a daughter mission church of St. Andrew's, Wiveliscombe, owned by the Rector and the Churchwardens.

2. Views of Huish Champflower.

3. Tuck Mill, is dated '1675 R G' which possibly stands for a member of the Govett family, who owned other mills in the area. Known as 'Took' mill in 1840, which suggests this was a tucking or fulling mill. The leat stream also served Jew's (D'Ewe's) Mill. (D and G).

4. Maundown Filter station, built in the 1960s and extended in the early 1970s, treats water from the nearby Clatworthy and Wimbleball reservoirs. This supplies around 200,000 people in central Somerset. From 2006 - 2009, £25 million will be spent to upgrade the water treatment facilities, the quality of the water and meet the increased demand for water in the area.

Huish Champflower Church

CIRCULAR WALK NUMBER 7

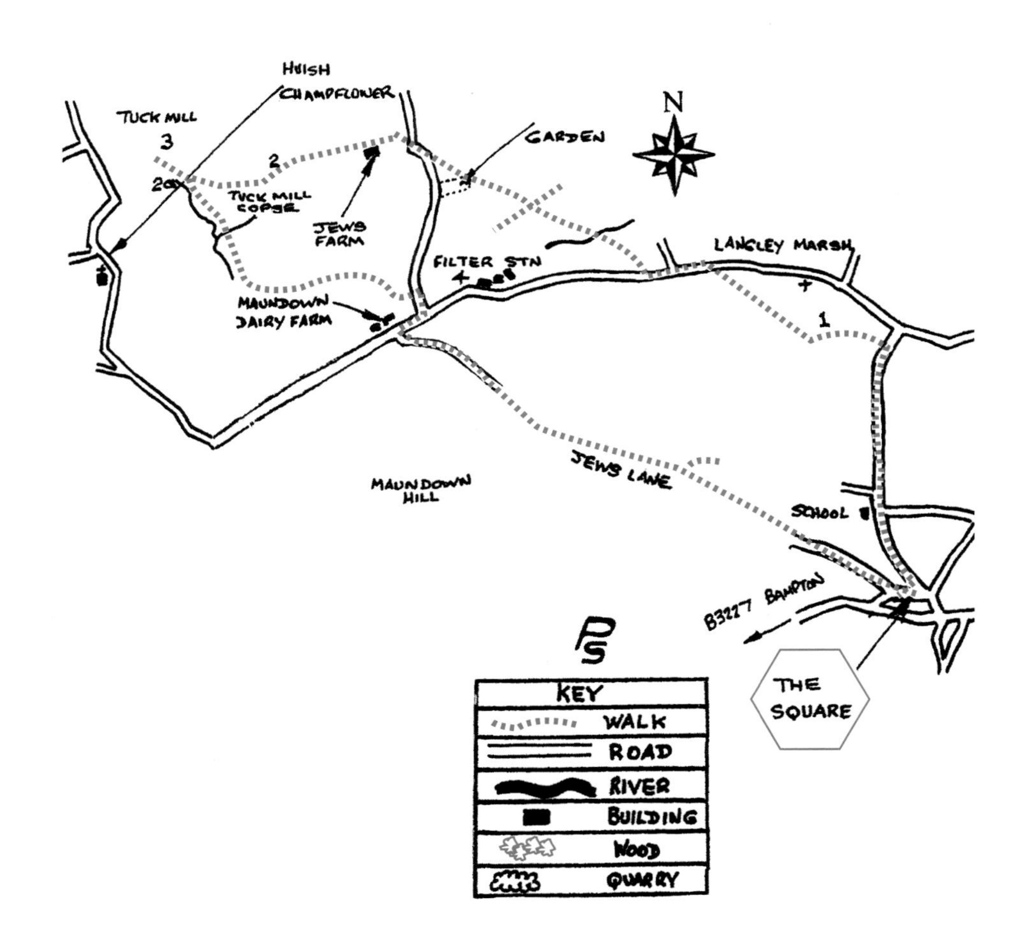

CIRCULAR WALK NUMBER 8

Wiveliscombe Square - The Old Reservoir - Jews Lane - Wiveliscombe Square

Time: 1/2 hr

Distance: 2 km (1 1/4 miles)

Map: OS pathfinder (1257) ST 0212 'Wellington' or OS Explorer 128 'Taunton and Blackdown Hills'.

Features: Track shaded by old beech trees in a valley to Wiveliscombe's original water supply which is now on private farm land. The buildings are in ruins and the actual reservoir almost completely overgrown. Children and dogs must be closely supervised in this area. Return on same track a short distance only. Then the path to The Square.

Grade: Very easy. One short, steep path.

Roadwalking: 250m/yds.

From Wiveliscombe Square, face The Pharmacy/White Hart Hotel and turn **left**. Continue to the junction with Croft Way and turn **right**. After 250m/yds turn **right** opposite the gates of the Wiveliscombe owned recreation ground. Follow the metalled road **(1)** which becomes a track **(2)**. Continue along this track for 1/2 km (1/4 mile) through the gate, ignore the track on the right **(3)** and continue to the next gate. This is the end of the public footpath. The reservoir is situated beyond this gate **(4)**. Retrace steps, (a little over 250m/yds) and go through the 'kissing gate' on the **left** onto a narrow fenced path. Continue through two stiles into a rough lane. (Jews Lane) Turn **right** and downhill. This soon becomes metalled and leads directly to Wiveliscombe.

POINTS OF INTEREST ON WALK 8

1. The house on the right was known as the 'Water Mill' this was a water grist mill, known as 'West Weare'. (D and G)

2. Quarry Cleeve, private land. On the right is the entrance to the disused quarry. (No access)

3. Fishponds on the left, in the field, provided the Hancock family, who lived at Quarry Cleeve with fresh fish. The ponds are no longer visible. (B)

4. The Reservoir supplied the brewery, the local community and swimming pool with water prior to the advent of Clatworthy Reservoir. (B and G)

CIRCULAR WALK NUMBER 8

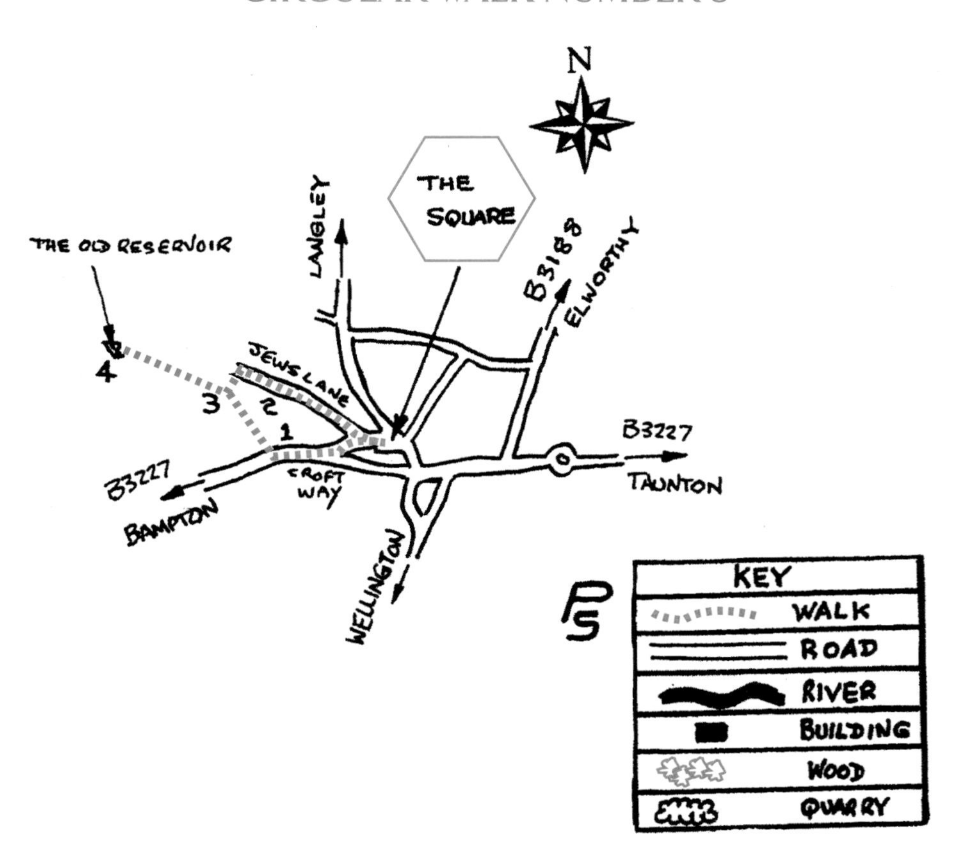

CIRCULAR WALK NUMBER 9

Wiveliscombe Square - Cutthroat Lane - Grant's Farm - Billy Farm - Deepleigh Lane - Yard Lane - Cutthroat Lane - Wiveliscombe Square

Time: $1\frac{1}{2}$ hrs

Distance: $4\frac{3}{4}$ km (3 miles)

Map: Pathfinder (1257) ST 02/12 'Wellington' or OS Explorer 128 'Taunton and Blackdown Hills'.

Features: Good views of Wiveliscombe and Oakhampton Quarry.

Grade: Easy. There is one moderate climb up a shady track with periodic views of Wiveliscombe. The walk is mostly on tracks and agricultural land, which can be muddy in wet weather.

Roadwalking: $\frac{1}{2}$ km ($\frac{1}{4}$ mile) on roads in Wiveliscombe and a short stretch of a minor lane.

From Wiveliscombe Square face The Pharmacy/White Hart and turn **right**. Walk ahead down Silver Street and Golden Hill. Turn **left** at the junction with Burges Lane and almost immediately **right** into a footpath **(1)**. Follow ahead to a stile into a field. Do not take the left-hand footpath. Continue straight ahead keeping the stream on the left. Continue through fields and two stiles, which are in the bottom left corners. The third stile is also in the bottom left corner but is easily missed, so keep close to the stream and avoid going uphill.

This last stile leads onto Grant's Lane. **. Turn **left** and walk over the bridge **(2)**. In about 100m/yds the lane bends sharply left but ignore this and continue straight ahead. Follow the fingerpost up a track, known as Billy Lane **(3)**. This is a steady uphill climb, of $^{1}/_{2}$ km ($^{1}/_{4}$ mile) **(4)**. The track bends right and descends steeply with deep ruts, until another track joins from the right **(5)**. Turn **left** for about 250m/yds and ignore another track, which joins from right. Continue a short climb, up Deepleigh Lane **(5a)**, then turn **left** down Sandy Lane for about 100m/yds. Follow the waymark through a gate on the left and leave Sandy Lane. Continue downhill, close to a hedge on the right. The path bends left and ascends slightly past an animal shed on the left **. Straight across the metalled lane, Grant's Lane, to a track, known as Yard Lane, and follow the fingerpost for 200m/yds, to a stile. **Right**, and descend through two fields to stiles in the bottom right corners. Follow the waymark half left in the next field. This field may be waterlogged and rough. The path is reinforced over the stream. Go over a stile into the next field then the final stile is a short distance on the **right**. Retrace steps through Cutthroat Lane and Golden Hill to Wiveliscombe Square.

POINTS OF INTEREST ON WALK 9

1. Cutthroat Lane. Legend relates a murder took place here in the 19th century. On the left is the site of the original Wiveliscombe Gas, Light and Coke Company (1857 - 1937). Towards the end of the lane on the left is one of the two sewerage works of Wiveliscombe.

2. In previous years a channel on the right was made to dip sheep.

3. There are many badger holes to be seen and evidence of cobbled/ cement roadways. This was another route from the Oakhampton quarry for hauling slate.

4. At this point, look left, for views of Langley. Look right to view 'Castle Hill', one of the Neolithic sites that run from North to South Somerset. Roman coins were found here which are now in the Somerset County Museum.

5. Oakhampton Quarry. The largest of the local quarries in the area. In 1608 the Dean and Chapter of Wells granted a lease to the Manor of Oakhampton, to develop the slate quarry. The Churchwardens' accounts show large quantities of slate were sold to the church for the roof. Alas, this slate was soft, nowadays imported slate is used. Some machinery, used in quarrying, is submerged at the bottom of the quarry. (B and G)

5a. Look right for another view of the quarry.

CIRCULAR WALK NUMBER 9

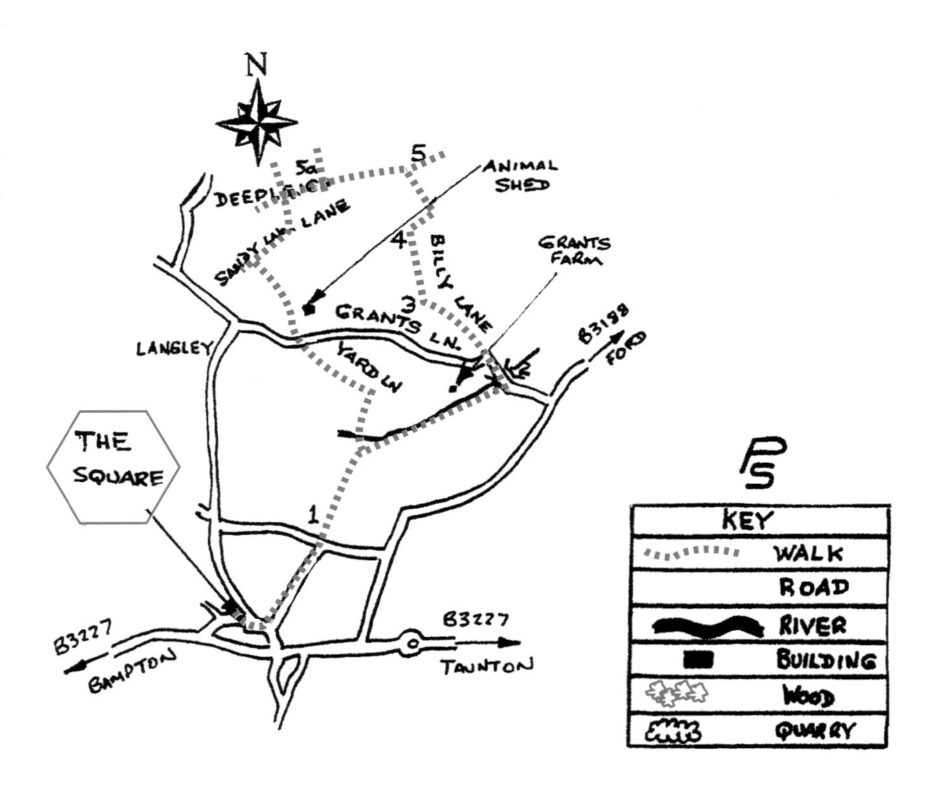

CIRCULAR WALK NUMBER 10
TOWN WALKS

Time: Variable

Distance: **First Walk:** 1 1/4 km (3/4 mile)
Second Walk: 2 km (1 1/4 miles)
Third Walk: 1 km (1/2 mile)

Features: The aim of these walks is to give an overall feel for this small, active community which was mentioned in the Domesday Book of 1086 and before but is now very much part of the twenty first century. The walk encompasses the different areas and most of the interesting buildings and sights of Wiveliscombe. These are numbered as they are passed and described briefly in 'the points of interest'. More details are to be found in the references.

Grade: Easy. Most of the walk is accessible for wheelchairs, the section which is not, is marked *.....**. Some of the hills in the Town make non-powered wheelchairs difficult and care must be taken due to the hills and also the uneven pavements.

Roadwalking: On roads, most of which have pavements. About 250m/yds is footpath, denoted *.....**.

First Town Walk

Face The Pharmacy/ White Hart and turn **right**, cross the road, into Silver Street. **(1)**. This road becomes Golden Hill, after passing Wyndham's flats on the left. **(2)** Beware of traffic. At the bottom of the hill turn **left** at the T junction, into Style Road, **(3)** continue into Northgate past Spring Gardens on the left and Plain Pond on the right. **(4)** Continue to the next T Junction at the top of Northgate, turn **left**, into North Street. **(5)** Continue past the car park into the Square.

Wiveliscombe Primary School

Points of interest on the First Town Walk

Silver Street (1)

a. Plaques are to be seen on buildings throughout the town, marking the sites of the old public houses. They were designed by various artists. Erected and funded by the Wiveliscombe Arts Consortium and the Jim Laker Fund in 2005.

b. 'The Old Reading Rooms' (1887) on the right, was also used as the Council Chamber for meetings until the early 1970's. (A and G)

c. One of the houses belonged to a Dr. Jonathan Gore Tudball, trained at Guy's Hospital, (1812 - 1813) who then joined Dr. Sully at the Dispensary. (B and G).

d. The Chapel, on the left, built in 1708, was the Congregational Church, now the Congregational Evangelical Alliance. This Chapel had a small graveyard, used since 1812 for worthy members of the chapel.

e. Wyndham Flats, on the left, was the site of the Wyndham family town house 400 years ago. At night it is reputed to resemble a lighted ship.(G)

Golden Hill (2)

a. The Mews on the right lead to the old brewery. The old counting house is on the left by the gates. The 'Bell House' is on the left hand side of Golden Hill, the bell was rung to call workers to the brewery and in case of fire. (G)

b. Borough House (No.15) note the pub plaque, 'the Cat and Fiddle'. This was the Court Leet, where Parish officers were based.

c. The site of the first Wesleyan Chapel in Wiveliscombe was behind number 29 (Ophir House). The congregation grew and a modern Chapel was erected in South Street in 1845, which is now the 'Chapel Gallery' (G)

d. Three storey tenement buildings, on the right, said to date from Napoleonic Times and reputed to have housed the Somerset Yeomanry (G)

e. Water hydrants in the wall can be seen between numbers 22 and 24 also at number 40. These were installed in the 1860s supplying water from local springs and the reservoir (See Walk 8). In the early 20th century the Wiveliscombe Urban District Council provided piped water to all households. (G and A)

f. Houses at the bottom of Golden Hill together with the now demolished Mason's Square (1963) on the right, were bequeathed by wealthy residents in the 16th century to raise money for the needy, now known as the Consolidated Charities Trustees. This Charity dispenses money to this day, to worthy elderly and to local organizations. (B and G)

Style Road (3)

a. Wiveliscombe Gas, Light and Coke Company (1857-1937) was on the right, past the footpath entrance. The gasometer was removed in 1966.

b. There is another water hydrant on the left.

Plain Pond (4)

a. This was a part of the Bishops estate and is believed to have provided fish for the Manor House. Houses were built here after the First World War and also in 1931.

North Street (5)

a. The Primary School, is on the right, note the entrances for boys and girls. This was the second school in Wiveliscombe, (1879), the first being the National School (1835) in the Church grounds.

b. 'Pulsford Lodge', on the left, is a purpose-built residential home named after a local family. (G)

c. The Old Police Station (1858), on the right, retains old 'lock ups' which are now part of the houses. A magistrates court was held here for minor offences. (G)

d. Richard Beadon Close, locally known as Rackclose, where woollen cloth after fulling and bleaching was laid out or racked to dry. Named after a Bishop of Bath and Wells and his son, who alienated the Manor of Wiveliscombe and Fitzhead in the 19th century. (B and G)

e. 'The Bear' a hostelry since the 18th century is on the left.

f. The site of the Market is through the arch by the garden shop. Regular markets took place here, cattle being herded through the streets, to and from the railway station. The market was demolished in 1984 to make way for an housing development.

Second Town Walk

Face The Pharmacy / White Hart, turn **left** walk towards the White Hart Hotel and West Street **(1)** continue past Jones' garage on the left until the main B3227 is reached, the bypass known as Croft Way. Cross the road turn **right**, walk approximately 30m/ 30yds, go through a gate on the left. **(2)**

Retrace steps to the road and turn **right** until a 'kissing gate' is reached on the right, walk down the path and go through the second 'kissing gate' turn **left**. Walk parallel to the house on the left, go through another gate and on to a metal road (South Street) **(3)** turn **right**, walk for 60m/70yds. to Beech Tree Close. Cross the road **(4)** and **left** into Russels, follow the narrow road for 120m /150 yds until a second door in the wall on the **right** is reached.

Go through this into the Churchyard **(5)**. To visit the church, go **left** to the North door. On leaving the Church turn **right**, to the East end, until a door is seen in the wall on the **left**, go through this door and look right **(6)**. Walk up track to the main road, **right**, **(7)** follow the pavement. **Right** into Station Road **(8)** follow road to a stile **(9)**.

Retrace steps to the main road. **Right** and follow the pavement **(10)** - Taunton Road - towards the roundabout, straight across the road, continue to walk on the verge to the 'Totems' **(11)**. Cross the road and return to the roundabout, **right** into Norden's Meadow, cross the road at the T junction and **left** after 100m/yds, **right**, into Lion D'Angers estate **(12)**.

The Wiveliscombe Memorial Recreation Ground

Follow the pavement around the green to a road junction, cross the road and ascend Old Brewery Road **(13) right**, before the houses and almost immediately **left** on to a cement steep road, follow this through the old Brewery Site **(14)** into Golden Hill and continue into the Square.

Points of interest on Second Town Walk

West Street (1)

a. The White Hart Hotel, built before 1800s, a Hancock establishment 'A respectable news room' in the 19th century (G).

b. The Jubilee Gardens (1977) built to commemorate the Queen's Silver Jubilee, where houses and shops once stood. The recent furniture, seats and gates were given by the Wiveliscombe Arts Consortium.

c. Prior to the construction of Croft Way (by pass) this road was the main route to North Devon, causing much frustration and stagnation of traffic, but also local financial gain!

The Memorial Recreational Ground (2)

This was given in memory to the fallen of the 1914-1918 War. It is still owned by the Wiveliscombe Parish Council. The Memorial Shelter was constructed in 1934, in memory of Froude Hancock, a local notable and also a rugby player for England. The rugby club was founded in 1872, possibly one of the oldest in England. The Cricket Club was founded in 1870, the football club circa 1908 and the tennis club in the 1920s. There is an outdoor swimming pool, opened in 1927, an envy of many local townships.

In 2005 new play equipment was erected, funds raised locally and from national grants.

South Street (3)

a. A terrace of 18th-19th century houses, on the right, known as Parricks Place after a former owner of the now demolished Temperance Hotel.

b. The Wesleyan Chapel on the left, is now an art gallery.

c. The Tanning Yard, was below the chapel, where water, lime, mastering and tan pits, together with other relevant buildings existed. The nearby fields are still called 'Tanners'. Houses now occupy the site (D and G).

Kingsmead School (4)

a. Built in the 1950's as a secondary school for 11-16 year old pupils, now noted for languages. This area was known as Lambrook.

b. The Lam Brook runs parallel to the school and joins the Millstream.

Church and surrounding buildings (5)

The gateway was an entry into the 16th century almshouses. The building on the left was the first school in Wiveliscombe (1835), this was known as the National School. The south windows are from the Bishop's Manor House (A and G).

b. The Church (1829) replaced a mediaeval church on the same site, demolished, as the tower was deemed unsafe and cracked. Information about the church and organ can be found inside (B).

c. The remains of a restored 14th century preaching cross base is on the north side of the church.

d. Few old gravestones are to be found, most being Victorian and later, due to the rebuilding of the church.

St Andrew's Church

The Archway (6)

This led into the Bishop's Manor (B and G).

Part of Church Street (7)

a. Bourne's House, on the left, built by Bishop Bourne in the 16th century boasts a fine plaster ceiling. The family were Royalists during the Civil War and suffered as a result. There are local legends of tunnels to the church and town, these possibly were old drains and conduits (B and G).

b. The modern Roman Catholic church is worth a visit, the former presbytery is next door, previously known as Westbourne.

c. The Masonic Hall, formerly Eastbourne, below the Church is a fine example of Regency architecture. Both these houses were built for Hancocks' senior staff. (G)

Station Road (8)

a. The station, on the left, was opened in 1871 and closed by Dr. Beeching in 1966. The passenger line ran from Taunton to Barnstaple and was also used to distribute agricultural produce and animals.

b. Bishop's Green (on the right) was the site of a tithe barn belonging to the Manor House (B and E).

The Mill Area (9)

a. The building on the right was originally a water mill owned by the Bishop where locals were obliged to grind their corn (grist mill) raising revenues for the Church (B and G).

b. A slaughter house and laundry were also to be found here, now converted into dwellings.

c. Note the old railway bridge and stream (The Mill stream, originating above Culverhayes and the old reservoir). (see Walk 8).

Tollgate (10)

a. The Tollgate at the junction of the Taunton and Watchet roads, was also an Inn, 'The Black Dog'

b. Ford Road was known as Frog Lane, because this was possibly boggy.

Entrance to Wiveliscombe (11)

a. The 'Totem poles' were commissioned by the Wiveliscombe Arts Consortium and represent trade, industry and leisure pursuits in the town. (2004) From left to right and top to bottom: **First column** - A green man, carvings as from local buildings, a tractor, sheep, a corn motif. **Second column** - A wyvern, reported to have flown around St. Andrew's Church, hanging slates/gables, rolls of Pennystone cloth, skittles. **Third column** - A Roman coin from Castle, a beer barrel, bottles related to brewing, rugby balls, rugby players and a winged cat.

b. The slate nameplate was given by the Twinning Association and opened by both French and local civic leaders (2005).

Lion D'Angers (12)

This was named after the twinned town in France. For twenty years visits have been made across the channel. The association continues to be active.

The Old Brewery site (13)

a. Founded by the Hancock family, (1807), after the collapse of the woollen trade, which had existed in the area for 400 hundred years, the brewery survived until 1959.

b. There are two smaller breweries in the town, one on the old site and the second in Ford Road. Both produce quality beers, which are widely distributed in the British Isles.

c. The malting house tower and chimney (1897) dominate the skyline.

Tunnels, cellars and passageways exist under the site. Possibly to avoid some excise tax (G).

Third Town Walk

Face The Pharmacy/White Hart **(1)** turn **right** to the corner of the Square, sharp **right** and cross the road into the High Street **(2)**. Follow road to the traffic lights. **Left** into Church Street. Cross the road before the Fish and Chip Shop and then follow the narrow steps down in to Rotton Row **(3)**. Follow the road ahead then turn **right** into Russel's **(4)** continue ahead to South Street and turn **right (5)**. Retrace steps, past the traffic lights into the High Street **(6)** to the Square.

Points of interest on Third Town walk

The Square (1)

a. This Square was redesigned in the 1980's allowing more pedestrian space and less parking.

b. Court House, built by the Hancock family in the 1880s, is decorated with timber and hanging tiles. Various carvings, including 'The Green Man ' can be seen.

The archway into the house is believed to have come from the Bishop's Manor.

c. London House, formerly 'The Bell Inn', another coaching house, now flats and shops.

Drain Steps

d. The Town Hall, (1845), the building with the clock, was designed by Richard Carver (who also designed the Church) and financed by the then Lord of the Manor, Lord Ashburton. This boasted a fine portico of pillars in the Market Square. The first markets were held in 1285 together with three fair days. In 1301 the town was made a Borough. The Reform Act (1832) demoted the status to a Urban Sanitary District (B and G).

The High Street or Town Hill, originally Fore Street

Going Downhill (Left hand side) (2)

a. The archway led into the amenities for the 'Lamb' Hotel/Inn, now known as Printers mews

b. Berrys, previously known as the 'Green Dragon' possibly a malt house and then a clothiers (G).

c. The Dispensary, (1804), founded by Dr. Sully, was the only hospital between Exeter and Bath at this period. This Doctor travelled throughout West Somerset and North Devon, administering to all. He is reputed to have enjoyed practical jokes. The building was used as a dispensary until the end of the 1939 - 1945 war. Part was used as a Doctors' surgery until 1986. The entire building is now flats.

Rotton Row (3)

a. These steps are known as 'Drain Steps', as water ran down here to join the Lam Brook, from a stone cistern/reservoir in Church Street.

b. Rotton Row is a corruption of the phrase 'Routine row'. Church processions followed this route

c. Gardens/allotments, on the left, over the wall, belong to the Church and are known as 'Caters', possibly a corruption of 'Caterers' as this belonged to the Bishop's Manor (B and G).

Russels (4)

a. This part of Russels originally was a private and cobbled road, with gates at either end. There is a masonry pier at the start of the road.

b. An old blacksmith and later a wheelwright's shop, on the right, was to be found at the junction with South Street,

South Street (5)

a. Known as the 'Gullet' due to the steep descent to Lam Brook. (Kingsmead School)

b. The new vicarage (rectory) is on the left; this replaced the old vicarage at the corner of South and Church Streets.

High Street (Going Uphill on the left) (6)

a. The 'Temperance Hotel' was demolished, together with the underpass to the old Vicarage to make way for the modern 'Croft Way' bypass.

b. 'The Courtyard Hotel', previously known as ' The Angel' is another coaching inn. In the rear was the revenue office.

c. Uppington's (1693) a Regency house

d. The 'Lion Hotel' with an archway leading to stables, where horses and coaches were housed. These are now shops and flats.

THE WIVEY WAY

Wiveliscombe Square - Washbattle - Bulland Ford - Waterrow - Hurstone Park - Waldridge Cross - Pyncombe Farm - Quarthill Lane - Sminhay Bridge - Screedy - Quaking House Lane - Slape Moor - Manor Cottages - Croford - Knight's Farm - Hoccombe - Burrow Hill Farm - Oakhampton Farm - Oakhampton Quarry - Whitefield - Jew's Farm - Tucks Mill - Huish Champflower - Maundown Hill - Wiveliscombe Square

Time: At least one long day's walk.

Distance: 36 km (23 miles)

Map: OS Pathfinder (1257) ST 0212 'Wellington' and Pathfinder ST 03/13 'Quantock Hills' or OS Explorer 128 'Taunton and Blackdown Hills' and OS Explorer OL9 'Exmoor'.

Features: This walk explores the varied terrain of this area. Pastures and agricultural land, gentle riverbanks, steep tracks, forestry and pheasant rearing, a nature reserve and a quarry. Wonderful panoramic views open up regularly. It only passes one pub or place for refreshment but with a short diversion others can be reached.

+.....++ indicates where The Wivey Way and West Deane Way follow the same route.

# denotes the point at which negotiations are underway to establish a right of access and public right of way over a railway bridge. At present follow the route as printed.

Grade: Difficult due to the quarry and length of walk. The quarry can be avoided by using open access between *.....***.

Roadwalking: 8½ km (5¼ miles). With the exception of a few short stretches this is on very minor lanes with wonderful views.

Return to Wiveliscombe: This is possible at several points denoted **. Reference is made to the circular walk in which the return is described. As all walks are written in an anti-clockwise direction it may be necessary to reverse the instructions. This is not difficult if reference is made to the OS map. If 'car' is mentioned, this is usually because the road is too busy for a pleasant walk.

Points of interest: These are numbered periodically and described at the end of the walk or reference is made to another walk where details may be found.

For points of interest see walk 1.

From Wiveliscombe Square face The Pharmacy/White Hart. Turn **left** into West Street. Take the first **right**, opposite Jones' garage, into a steep lane with high hedges. At the end of the metalled lane a driveway leads to Quarry Cleeve **(1)**. Follow the signpost on the right pointing ahead. Climb for ¾ km (½ mile). Ignore a track on the right **(2)** + **. Continue to climb. At the road junction, turn sharp **left** and follow a footpath sign in the left hedge. Continue along the track. Stop at the gaps on the left **(3)**.

Ignore a metal gate ahead. The track bends right. As it bends left (100m/yds) stop at the bend and look over the gate **(4)**. Continue along the track for 250m/yds and go through the gate ahead. Keep the hedge on the **right** for 70m/yds then go through the first gate on the right into a field. Walk ahead. As the field drops steeply look towards the right for a metal gate. Go through this gate into the forestry land. Follow the Deane Way signs to a metal road. Beware of the traffic ahead **(car). Turn **left** along the road to a track just before a bridge **(5)**. Turn **left** along this track for 1 1/4 km (3/4 mile), through the forestry land, with the River Tone on your right. Go past the houses on your left and through a gate until a gamekeeper's cottage (where geese may be kept) is reached on the left. This area is Bulland Ford ** (Walk 1).

For points of interest see walk 2.

Cross the road, but keep the river and the ford on the right, to a footbridge. Cross the river by this bridge then bear **left** with the river on the left. A waymark is found a little way down this path. **Please keep dogs on leads as pheasants are bred in the area**. Continue ahead, about 3/4 km (1/2 mile), to a barn and farm on the left. Turn **right** here and climb uphill. Turn **left** at the junction and look for a gate in the hedge on your left. Go through this gate and down a track to another gate, then **right** to reach a metalled road. Turn **right** again for 1 1/4 km (3/4 mile). Ignore the roads on the right, and go straight on to reach The Rock Inn **(5)** at Waterrow **(6)** **(car or bus) ++.

From The Rock cross the main B3227 and turn **left**, over the bridge, then immediately **right** to the car park and continue on this lane, signed to Hurstone, with the river on your right. As the road bends left, in about 250m/yds, look right for a 'V' shaped stone entrance also on the right. Go **right** through this into Hurstone Nature Reserve **(7)** and continue uphill with the river on the right. Follow the fenced footpath through several fields. Walk on the left of a wooden seat and ignore a path going downhill on your right **(8)**. Continue on the path **(9)**, which bends sharply left uphill to a metal gate.

There is a pond ahead. Go round this on either side. Continue uphill with the stream on the right through a lightly wooded area. Up flights of wooden steps into a field **(10).** Turn **right**, with the hedge on the right and fence on the left, to a gate in the top right corner of the field. Go through this onto the lane and leave the Nature Reserve. Turn **right** along the lane and then **left** at the junction, and follow the sign 'Bathealton' to crossroads in about 250m/yds **(11)**. Turn **left** and follow the sign to Wiveliscombe. Continue on the lane, for 250m/yds, to a barn on the left then go immediately **left** up the bridleway. Climb and admire the views **(12)**. The track then descends to a metalled lane at Waldridge Cross **(13)**. **(walk 2). Turn **left** along the lane, which soon bends right. At this point turn **right** over a stile.

Follow the footpath sign across the field in the direction of the poles. Go through a gate and keep the hedge on your left and then through another gate. In a short distance turn **left** into a small field. Keep the farm buildings on your right and walk ahead to a track. Turn **right**. Walk past all the buildings. Then go **right**, through a gate, into a small field. Continue ahead with the hedge on your right.

Descend into a small, brambly spinney with a boggy stream at the bottom and a wall ahead. Turn **right** and cross the stream. Go through a gate into a field. Continue ahead, in the steep- sided valley, with the river on the right, walk through several rough fields and woodland. Take care in the woods, as there may be low wire fences associated with the pheasant shoot. The direction is basically unchanged. Go through a large metal gate into a field, with woodland on the left and the river right.

As the field opens up bear **left** uphill, away from the river to a stile in the top left corner. Go over the stile and turn **left** along the edge of the field. The path cuts off the top edge of this field and passes to a gate opposite. Go through this gate and turn **right** into Quarthill Lane. **(walk 3 in reverse)

For points of interest see walk 3.

Quarthill Lane **(4)** continues for about 1 km (1/2 mile). Then it bends uphill to a metalled lane **(car). Turn **left** and go under Sminhay Bridge **(5)**, then **left** again along a lane. Past three properties on the left. As the lane bends sharply left look for a signpost on the right, and follow it, **right**, through a gate to Poole Farm **(6)**. Follow the waymarks carefully through this private estate. Your direction is ahead. Leave a pond and hedge to the left. In about 100m/yds turn **left**, through a gap in the hedge and over a wooden bridge, which may be slippery when wet.

Walk ahead, past a pole on the left, over another stream and continue ahead between two ponds. The path bears **left** into shrubland and passes over another wooden bridge. Continue ahead over the field and some roofs will appear. Keep these to the right and go over a stile onto the road. Turn **right** along the grass verge, for 20m/yds, to avoid walking on the Wiveliscombe to Wellington road. **(car). Cross the road and turn **left**, at Ivy Cottage. Continue on this lane 250m/yds. As the lane bends sharp right, look for a signpost on the left. Turn l**eft**, through a metal gate. The footpath is ahead to a stile opposite . Go over the stile, which may be slippery.

Turn **right** to the right-hand corner of the field and cross the bridge over a stream. Go over another stile and climb the hilly field, through a gate, to the stile in the top right corner. Go over this stile **(7)** and walk along the top edge of the next field with the hedge on the left. The buildings of Farthing's Farm are to the right. Follow the track as it bends sharply **left**. At the junction of tracks turn **left** uphill between hedges. The track joins a metalled lane **(8)** **(car). Turn **left (9)** and walk about 1/2 km (1/4 mile).

Look for a footpath sign on the left and turn **left**, through the gate and walk across the field, slightly to the right, to a stile opposite. Go over this stile. Beware of possible knee-high electric wire on the opposite side of the stile and the use of temporary electric wire in the next three fields. Keep the row of four white cottages almost straight ahead and continue to a metal gate. Cross the lane and go through the gate opposite. Walk straight across the next field, with the four cottages directly ahead, and through a gap in the hedge opposite to descend to the bottom left corner of the field. Go through a metal gate and ahead into a small spinney.

Cross the wooden bridge over Hillfarance brook. Turn **left** along the bank with the brook to the left. Wiveliscombe is directly ahead **(10)**. Where the brook goes into a tunnel the permissive path turns 90 degrees **right**. Follow this to the main B3227 and cross the road **(car). The road is busy but this crossing point gives good visibility on both sides. #. Turn **left** along the wide grassy verge and follow this in the direction of Wiveliscombe to the roundabout, then turn **right** into Nordens Meadow then first left into Lion D'Angers **(11)** ** (walk 3). Turn **right** and follow the pavement around the edge of the houses. At the top of the green turn **right** to the very top of the estate and go over a stile into a track, known as Newton's Lane. Turn **right** along this and go through a kissing gate at the end. Follow the well - worn footpath towards the pole at the top of the field. Continue, with the hedge on your left, to a stile.

Go over the stile and immediately **right**, around the edge of the field with the hedge on the right. Descend a small hill to a gate. Go through this, over the track and through another gate opposite.

For points of interest see end.

Follow the footpath around the edge of Hyden Wood and Castle Hill. Go through gates and stiles for about 1/2 km (1/4 mile) until a metalled lane is reached **(1)** **(car). Turn **right** down the lane to a ruined railway bridge **(2)**, then **left** up Croford Hill for just under 1 km (1/2 mile).

Follow the sign **left** up the bridleway, Cat's Ash Lane **(3)**. Climb uphill initially and continue for about 3/4 km (1/2 mile) , until a metalled lane is reached. Turn **left**. Keep on this lane and ignore a lane on the right, walk past a farm and houses on your left and continue until a road joins from the right **(4)**. Do not take this but continue **left** and follow the sign to Wiveliscombe. In 50 m/yds turn **right** and follow the sign to Hoccombe, over a stile and keep the hedge on your right. Go through a squeezer stile ahead **(5)**, then slightly **left**, across the field, and head directly towards Willett Tower **(6)** on the skyline.

Go through another squeezer stile in the hedge. Walk straight ahead and keep a large clump of trees, in the dip, on the left. Go through the squeezer stile, in the middle of hedge opposite and over a humpback bridge, then straight across the field, and through a gate onto a metalled lane. Turn **left** and walk for about 1/2 km (1/4 mile) to Hoccombe hamlet **(7)**. Just beyond the property, known as Hoccombe Barn, follow the footpath **left**, close to the farm buildings, and over a bridge and small stile. Keep the hedge on the left and head for another bridge and stile. Go over these, with the hedge still on the left, to a stile in the top left corner of this field.

Turn **left** on the road. Walk on the road around Burrow Hill Farm **(8)** and take the first **right twice** so that the farm is always on the right.

Continue along this lane for just over 1 km (3/4 mile) to the road from Wiveliscombe **(car). Turn **right** and walk on the grass verge, for about 50 m/yds. Cross the road and turn **left.** Follow the footpath sign up the track to Oakhampton Farm. Leave the house on the left, and walk straight ahead through a gate between farm buildings. Follow the track around the buildings then bear **right** through another gate.

For points of interest see walk 5.

Continue to a junction of several gateways. Take the first right into a field and keep the hedge on your left. The track bends left. Continue close to the hedge and go through another gate ahead. Climb the stile in the left corner of this field. Cross the next field and keep slightly to the right of centre. At the top of a slight incline keep left of an attractive 'shipham barn' for sheep **(5)**. The slate quarry **(6)** is visible, in the distance, a little to the left. Continue in the same direction over the stile at the corner of the wood ahead and into the quarry area. A 'caution' sign is a reminder that care must be observed at all times with dogs on leads and children under control. Continue straight ahead until a waymark indicates that the footpath bends sharp left.

To avoid the quarry face ** go straight ahead and follow the OS map through the wooded area, which contains well-established tracks to which the landowner has given access to walkers. The direction is downhill and to the **left** until a wide track is reached. Turn **left** and look for a low red cautionary sign on the right in about 250m/yds. Turn sharply **right** to complete the quarry descent. This is narrow and steep ***.*

To continue The Wivey Way down the main quarry face follow the marked path left into a clearing. (Do not turn right at this point as this path drops into the quarry in a short distance). The footpath continues ahead. The direction is in line with a cottage in the valley and is steeply downhill. It can be hazardous due to loose slate. Extreme caution is required here, until a wide flat path is reached. Turn **right** and follow the track until a waymark (on a low metal sign) is seen on the left. Turn **left** and descend steeply. *** Care must still be exercised. At the bottom of the quarry cross the stream and stile. Keep the hedge on your right. Go over the stile in the top right corner of the field and turn **left**. The track bends right and climbs steeply.

For points of interest see end

Just after the track starts to descend and bends left there is a steep bank, stile and footpath sign on the **right**. Go over this stile and ahead, across the field and over the next stile. There may be an electric wire at this point. Walk ahead, across the field, towards trees in the hedge and go through the gate. Continue straight on with the hedge on the left. Go through the next gate, past a tennis court on the right and Whitefield House on the left to a metalled lane **. Turn **left**, then fork **right** along Blackwater Lane for under 1/2 km (1/4 mile).

Tuck Mill

Just past a bungalow on the right, turn **right**, over a stile, and follow the footpath sign ahead, across the field, to another stile opposite. Go over this stile and continue to where a footpath and a small stream cross the path and a stile will be found on the right before a gate ahead. Turn **right**, over this stile, head up the field and through a gate at the top. Turn immediately **right** through another gate and cross the field to a stile in the left hedge. This leads into a beautiful private garden.

Continue ahead (through the garden) keep the house on the left and greenhouse on the right. Climb over the stile ahead, past a shed and house (close on the right) into a metalled lane, Jews Lane **. Cross this lane into the driveway of Jews Farm.

Go past the house on the left, to a gate, onto a track. Turn **left**. The houses and farm buildings are on the left. Go through two more gates into a field. Go straight across the first field to a gate. Walk slightly to the left across the next field, with Huish Champflower Church directly ahead, then through the left of two gates. Walk ahead through the next field, which may have a small stream in the middle of it, but do not descend the hill to the bottom. Go through a metal gate into a gorse thicket.

The path leads downhill, through a wooded area, for a little less than 250m/yds until the ruined Tuck Mill **(9)** appears ahead. Do not go as far as the mill but turn sharp **left**, then **right** over an iron bridge and continue ahead.

Walk past outbuildings and follow the track to the road.**(car) Turn **left** and follow the road into Huish Champflower. Walk 1/2 km (1/4 mile) along the road (ignore the road on the right) to the Church **(10)**. A few hundred m/yds past the Church on your left, note Gauth House **(11)**, said to be the oldest house in Huish Champflower. Turn **left**, into the driveway of Gauth House, walk ahead for 15m/yds and through a small gate.

Turn immediately **right** follow the wall at the back of Gauth House on the right, then through a metal gate ahead into a field. Turn **left** for 25m/yds and then **right** across the field to a double stile opposite. Go over this and continue in the same direction, across the field to the top left corner and junction of three gates. Walk **ahead**, through two of these gates, (ignore the gate on the right), straight on for 20m/yds and turn **right** through a gate in the hedge.

Turn **left** downhill to the bottom left corner of the field, then ahead into a small field with a stile opposite. Go over this, and a bridge over the millstream from Tuck Mill. Walk ahead, close to the left hedge, until a stile is reached. Turn **left** to climb this stile and immediately **right**, with the hedge on the right, to the right hand corner of the field. Go through a gate and along the track to the road ** (car)

For a shorter route *turn **left** and take the first turning **right**, (after a saw mill) follow the road, (note the garden on the right) to the top of Maundown. Keep on the track (Jew's Lane) and return to Wiveliscombe Square.*

To continue the Wivey Way turn **right** and walk on the road for 250m/yds. Follow the signpost **left** in the hedge into forestry land. Follow the 'Deane Way' way marks to Maundown hill and drop down into Wiveliscombe and the Square, by way of Jew's lane. This route was followed at the beginning of the walk The 'Wivey Way' is now completed.

Points of interest on the Wivey Way

1. Castle Hill. One of a chain of Neolithic Forts running from the North to the South of Somerset. Composed of sand, lime and pebbles from the Triassic period. Legends related caves were used here for escapes from marauding hordes but disproved. The flat hilltop summit is 12 acres (5Ha) with an almost complete fosse (ditch) except where lime-kilns intrude on the northerly side. Vestiges of fortifications can be traced. It has been occupied from Neolithic times including Bronze, Iron Age, Celts, Romans and Saxons. Artifacts, substantiating this, are to be found in the Somerset County Museum, Taunton. Roman coins were found in 1711 and 1946, including a Roman cameo brooch. The site is a protected ancient monument (B, E and G).

2. The Taunton to Barnstaple Railway. (F and G)

3. Cat's Ash, 'The wild cat's ash tree' from the old English 'calt' and aesc.' Possibly traceable to the idea of boundary trees. (C)

4. Diversion to Fitzhead and the public house. Fizthead in old English meaning 'The hide of a she fox' (C)

5. View of Quantocks.

6. Willett Tower, possibly built as a hunting lodge, or a folly, or an observation look out to check on employees. From the Old English 'wilitit' meaning 'full of willow '. (C)

7. Hoccombe from the old English meaning 'Curved Valley' The family of Hancocks had a fulling mill here in the 16th century. (B and C)

8. Lime Kilns produced top quality agricultural lime until 1901

9. Tuck Mill is dated '1685 RG' which possibly stands for a member of the Govett family, who owned other mills in the area. Known as 'Took'mill in 1840, which suggests this was a tucking mill or fulling mill. The leat stream also served Jew's (d'Ewe's) mill. (D and G)

10. Huish Champflower, in the Domesday Book of 1086, is listed as 'Hiwis' or house. From 1166 landowner's names such as Da Compo Florido and later Matilda De Chamflur were corrupted giving the present name to the village. St. Peter's Church is first mentioned in 1226, the main church is 15th century. A Robert Norton between 1410-40 cast one of the bells in Exeter. More details are obtainable in the Church. (The Church key may be obtainable from Church Cottage).

11. Gauth House (1450) is reputed to be a traditional mediaeval house, the last extensions being added in the 18th century.